S0-BNV-690

Lutheran DNA

Lutheran DNA

Testing the Augsburg Confession in the Parish

JAMES G. COBB

Dot,

Thank you for all you do via Ascension. Your partnership in ministry is wonderful. Blessings, Pastor J—

RESOURCE *Publications* · Eugene, Oregon

LUTHERAN DNA
Testing the Augsburg Confession in the Parish

Copyright © 2010 James G. Cobb. All rights reserved. Except for brief
quotations in critical publications or reviews, no part of this book
may be reproduced in any manner without prior written permission
from the publisher. Write: Permissions, Wipf and Stock Publishers,
199 W. 8th Ave., Suite 3, Eugene, OR 97401.

Resource Publications
An Imprint of Wipf and Stock Publishers
199 W. 8th Ave., Suite 3
Eugene, OR 97401
www.wipfandstock.com

ISBN 13: 978-1-60899-357-4

Manufactured in the U.S.A.

Material of the Augsburg Confession are taken from *The Book
of Concord*, translated by Robert Kolb and Timothy J. Wengert.
Copyright 2000 Fortress Press. Reproduced by special permission of
Augsburg Fortress.

Contents

SPECIFIC ABUSES ADDRESSED

Acknowledgments

THERE ARE so many people I wish to thank for my life's journey with the Augsburg Confession as a special part of my faith biography. To parents, Rev. James K. and Ellen W. Cobb, who nurtured me in Lutheran faith; to my wife Rev. Judith A. Cobb, who lives gospel joy daily and reflects the grace of Jesus; to sons, Christopher and Stephen who have some of this formation in their DNA as well; to colleagues at Lutheran Theological Seminary, Gettysburg, Pa. (1999–2006), faithful in their callings; to Drs. Eric Gritsch and Robert Jensen, wonderful and profound teachers; but especially to the parishes I have served and their interest in these matters: St. Martin, Annapolis, MD. (1973–74); Christ, Fredericksburg, VA. (1974–81); Trinity, Grand Rapids, MI. (1981–88); First, Norfolk, VA (1988–99) and Ascension, Towson, MD (2006–). It is especially in congregations where these matters live!

This manuscript was completed with a special sabbatical appointment from Graduate Theological Foundation, Dodge House, Mishawaka, IN., which designated me as an "Oxford Foundation Fellow," allowing me special library privileges at Bodleian Library, Oxford University, England, thus assuring the completion of this manuscript. Thanks to Ascension Lutheran Church Towson, MD, for sabbatical time and to the Graduate Theological Foundation for special appointment and to Ellen Persons for assisting with formatting.

Preface

Augsburg, Germany, June 25, 1530. This public reading of the "Lutheran" declaration of faith enters the annals of history. Emperor Charles V had summoned an imperial diet hoping to end the religious disunity throughout his lands. The princes and representatives of free cities were invited to make a presentation of their religious beliefs in the hopes of restoring unity. Thus, the elector of Saxony asked his Wittenberg theologians to begin preparation of such a document. This Lutheran statement certainly has the imprint of Martin Luther and Philip Melanchthon but its signatures would be from laity, not theologians: seven princes and representatives of two free cities! Historians tell a story of all the intrigue connected with political, religious and geographic events of the era. Many theologians will forever use the declaration as a springboard for biblical and doctrinal dialogue and debate. But how do some of the issues continue to surface in the life of congregations and parishioners? Every pastor could write some commentary about this. I choose to reflect on some of my pastoral experiences of parish life through the lens of this great confession of the church. In doing so, I have used the "Book of Concord," (Robert Kolb/Timothy Wengert Edition, 2000, reproduced by special permission of Augsburg Fortress Publishers) with the English translation of the Latin text. Also, I have omitted the sections of the commentary on the texts dealing with the "condemnations" found within most of the articles; they are worthy of separate study and commentary. I will forever remember my two outstanding teachers of Lutheran Confessions at Lutheran Theological Seminary at Gettysburg: Eric Gritsch and Robert Jenson. They made these documents come alive with clarity in their teaching and lively debate among students. The issues contained in the Augsburg Confession should continue to guide and inform congregational life among those who identify themselves as "Lutheran." To such congregations and persons, these words are offered.

James G. Cobb
Baltimore, Maryland

Overview of the Augsburg Confession

D r. Eric Gritsch, Reformation historian and professor at Gettysburg Seminary, wrote a series of commentaries on the Confession for the "Central Pennsylvania Focus" edition of the <u>Lutheran</u> on the occasion of the 450 anniversary of the Confession beginning in the Spring of 1980. With the writer's permission, portions of that over-view are printed here:

"Philip Melanchthon's draft had three objectives:

1. to show that Lutherans agree with the teachings of the ancient church (marked by the dogma of the Trinity in the Nicene Creed of 325 A.D.);

2. to propose doctrinal reforms based upon the understanding of the Gospel as God's promise of unconditional love ("justification by grace through faith without works of law") and

3. to make a proper distinction between doctrines essential to the life of the Gospel and teachings which tend to abuse the Gospel (Parts 1 and 2 of the confession).

All 28 articles of the Augsburg Confession are guided by a specific proposal of dogma made by Lutherans to the church catholic: *the church must create sufficient space for such preaching, teaching and acting that what is said, heard and done communicates God's unconditional love disclosed in a child-like trust by his creatures ("faith") rather than a conditional love disclosed in a calculating system of merit whereby salvation is earned ("works").*

Articles 1–4 stress the agreement with the Trinitarian creeds that sinful creatures are reconciled to God through Christ who alone has done satisfaction for sin.

Articles 5–15 describe how trust in Christ's work for human salvation is obtained and nurtured in the world: the ministry of the "audible" and "visible words"—word and sacraments—in, through and by the church as the gathering around the Gospel.

Article 16 affirms the functional interaction of church and state.

Article 17 anticipates the second coming of Christ.

Articles 18–20 teach that moral deeds follow faith rather than cause it.

Article 21 rejects the cult of the saints as a means to gather merit before God.

Articles 22–28 list the "abuses which have been corrected" by Lutherans in their territories: they give bread *and* wine to lay persons (22); they affirm the marriage of priests (23); they celebrate the mass albeit in such a way as to avoid works righteousness (24); they practice private confession without plaguing consciences with casuistry (25); they reject fasting and monastic vows as meritorious "works" (26–27); and they retain the office of bishop as long as bishops do not betray the Gospel (28)." (Gritsch, op. cit., with author's permission).

Further, the historic trajectory of this document moved into other venues in the years following its initial presentation. Writing in 1980, Roman Catholic theologian, Dr. Avery Dulles said that everything in the C.A. (Confession of Augsburg) was considered (by its writers), to be in agreement with the faith of the one catholic church. "Therefore, the C.A. is, in principle, an ecumenical document." He goes on to speak of its impact:

> Melancthon composed a variant form of the C.A. (Confessio Variata) for the Swiss reformers and this was accepted by Calvin in 1541. At the Peace of Westphalia (1648), the Calvinist reformation was recognized as belonging to the family of the C.A. In England, Thomas Cranmer derived many of the forty-two articles from the C.A., and in this way it became one of the major sources

for the thirty-nine articles of the Church of England.
Thus, the three main branches of the Reformation are in
different ways indebted to the C.A.[1]

There are many fine scholarly and academic commentaries
on the Augsburg Confession. This writing is not meant to be in
that vain. It is a parish pastor's reflection on some of the implications, practicalities and trajectories of parish life and congregational issues realizing that some such moments in ministry
remain, to this day, grounded in the Reformation's good soil of
grace and faith.

Southern Seminary staff colleague, John Largen, shared
a story making its rounds that may begin this writing with an
interesting image. The story is about a little boy who goes to the
corner grocery store to buy a box of laundry detergent. "How
much is this?" the young boy asks the clerk. "What are you going
to do with that large box?" asks the clerk. The boy responds, "I'm
gonna wash my cat." "Wash your cat? You shouldn't wash your
cat with that soap. It's much too strong." But the boy insisted on
the purchase. When he returned in a few days, the clerk couldn't
wait to ask about the cat. "Oh," said the boy, "the cat died." "Sorry
to hear that but I warned you not to use laundry detergent," said
the clerk. "Aw, the soap didn't hurt him," the boy replied. "It was
the spin cycle that got him." Depending on perspectives, some
may think that the Reformation was a washing and cleansing.
Others will think that the spin cycle was truly a whirlwind in history churning everything towards both a dying and a birthing.

May readers wander around for a while in an important
confessional document, reflect on the implications within each
congregation's life, and consider the cleansing and the spinning
that derives from an important historical and foundational
confession.

1. Dulles cited in Burgess, "The Role of the Augsburg Confession,"
131.

"Concerning God"

The churches among us teach with complete unanimity that the decree of the Council of Nicaea concerning the unity of the divine essence and concerning the three persons is true and should be believed without any doubt. That is to say, there is one divine essence, which is called God and is God: eternal, incorporeal, indivisible, of immeasurable power, wisdom, and goodness, the creator and preserver of all things, visible and invisible. Yet, there are three persons, coeternal and of the same essence and power: the Father, the Son, and the Holy Spirit. And the term "person" is used, for that meaning which the church's authors used in this case: to signify not a part or quality in another but that which subsists in itself.

CHRONIC CONFUSIONS pop up in conversations about God! In the United States, one never knows what the term means in any particular conversation. To the atheist, there is *no* God. To the agnostic, it's a "*maybe/maybe not* question." To the "survey in the street" audience, God may be the spouse of "mother nature." And, to many others, there is the generic "god-bless-America." This god alone, protects the U.S.A, a capitalistic democracy and does not include other nations and cultures! (So what have all those previous centuries of other national arrangements done with the Christian faith?).

1

Then there is the "god must be whatever any old or new religion espouses God is" crowd (i.e., "let's be tolerant and nice to every one crowd.") God is an optional product on a grocery shelf where you select your God product according to the packaging, ingredients and appeal in your own "heart of hearts." Americans have such a short grasp of history and therefore tradition. As Gerald Christiansen said in a convocation address, "many people think that all significant history began on their own personal birth date."[1] The larger picture is needed: a whole sweep of salvation history back to Genesis/Exodus. A revelation from God to us begins the whole process (see the very gift character of this order . . . revealed *from* God to us; not our thoughts, our conclusions, our insights): try these statements on for size:

- In the beginning, God . . .

- I am who I am . . .

- I am the God who delivered you from Pharaoh and led you out . . .

- I am the God of Abraham, Isaac and Jacob . . .

- God is the One who raised Jesus from the dead . . .

These contemplations are too huge to ever exhaust! But they present something for us to ponder: God reveals, God acts, God chooses, God delivers, God saves, God leads and guides (think of other verbs to fill in the blank). God is chief actor, not us. God is the subject of all things. God reveals and discloses. "God" is known in action verbs and in the doing of mighty deeds. Many of us have had late night "bull sessions" from teen youth retreats to college tavern talks about God. Is there a God? Is there evidence? Does evidence convince or do we instead stand on the borders of something called "faith?" For Christians, this discussion moves on to the One called

1. "Convocation Address," given at Lutheran Theological Seminary at Gettysburg, 2005.

"JESUS"

An oft used sermon illustration gives us a good handle on the understanding of incarnation. Here it is.

"A child has been put to bed by parents. A huge lightning bolt flashes and the child hears crashing thunder. The child stands at the top of the stairs calling down, "hey, I'm scared." The parent says, "it's ok now, go back to bed." Back in bed, another boomer, and the child calls out, "Hey everybody, I'm scared." Parents respond, "Just remember, God is with you so go back to bed and say a prayer." A moment later and a house-rocking thunder clap explodes and the child's quick scream, "I know God is with me but I'd like to see somebody with skin on, up here, now!"

"And the Word became flesh and dwells among us full of grace and truth." In the sweep of God's covenant, there came to be an embedded promise in prophecy that a Messiah would come. Such longing and such hope continued for centuries and generations. So, annually, our world is affected and influenced by a season of the Church gone commercial called Christmas. In my parish ministry, I have made one significant liturgical innovation (amid hundreds of minor ones). On Christmas Eve/day, I place the chalice and loaf in the manger. Children get it, some adults don't notice. 'What's in the manger?' Bread and Wine. Jesus is present for us, Jesus is our Christmas present. The Festival of the Incarnation was not an easy time to bring "incarnation" in bread and wine as the central focus of the church's worship celebration. The altar guild has tried to sabotage the effort with "we have always banked the chancel area with poinsettias; we can't have Communion that night!" It took quite a congregational council debate to spring that one into the parish's life! Scripture's story continued to move along from God and creation to Jesus and incarnation of the Word. And then,

"Holy Spirit"

I have heard the Holy Spirit used to justify so many cockamamie ideas that I remain cautious and careful in discerning what is of the "spirit" and what is not. Compounding the problem also is a literal explosion of things "spiritual" to the point that book stores now have sections devoted to spirituality, spiritual direction and spirit this and spirit that. I heard a parishioner stand up in a congregational meeting that was having a factious time about a possible call candidate and announce that it seemed that the Holy Spirit was directing her group toward this particular person; the problem was that the Bishop, seated in that meeting, and with the backing of church policy, said "no" to this; so where was the Holy Spirit? Do we invoke a spiritual baptism of our ideas? Does the Spirit work only in majority votes or by papal decree or in forming consensus? Frederick Buechner writes about all kinds of "spirits."[2] He writes that there are all kinds of spirits: school spirit, the American spirit, the Christmas spirit. Of the Holy Spirit, he writes that God is the power of life itself; God has breathed and continues to breathe God's self into God's creation. Jesus said that the Spirit would guide us into the way of truth. Deciding about "that" sometimes takes an accumulation of time and history and distance to pronounce it so (20/20 hindsight!). But I like another cue that Jesus gives us when he says, "the Spirit will bear witness to me" (John 15: 26). Here the Holy Spirit is called "counselor," and the Spirit's role will be to convince the world of sin, righteousness and judgment (John 16: 7–8). The task of the Holy Spirit is to bring to remembrance all that Jesus is and has said, taught and done *and* is doing now *and* will be doing in the future, according to the very same Jesus, resurrected and living!

Frank Senn in *Christian Liturgy*, puts it like this:

2. Buechner, *Wishful Thinking*, 90–91.

> . . . the Spirit is the link, as it were, between the divine community of God in three persons and the human community, comprised of persons created in the likeness of this God and then re-created in the likeness of the Son in Holy Baptism. The Spirit is the source of mission because the Spirit works through the preaching of the gospel of Jesus Christ and the administration of the sacraments of Christ. . . . Gregory Dix reminds us, the Spirit is the power or presence of the risen and ascended Jesus energizing his body, the church. The Spirit's function is to link the believers with the first and last comings of Christ and to constitute the church as the eschatological community, the first fruits of the new creation. [3]

(I must admit to never having had a late night conversation about the "Trinitarian hypostasis," perhaps missing that bull session in seminary, but there have been plenty of conversations about the American penchant for "modalism" or breaking the Trinity into parts).

Questions for Reflection

- The Name of "God" is invoked in everything from national policies to civic clubs to golf course openings. Is there a time when this is inappropriate?

- In inter-faith discussions, is the particularity of "Jesus" given up in discussions between mono-theistic and Trinitarian faiths?

- Do the three articles of the Apostles' Creed help in clarifying the name and work of the three personas of our One God?

- What has been your understanding of how one discerns the work of the Holy Spirit?

3. Senn, Christian Liturgy, 39–40.

Article 2

"Concerning Original Sin"

Likewise they teach that since the fall of Adam all human beings who are propagated according to nature are born with sin, that is without fear of God, without trust in God, and with concupiscence. And they teach that this disease or original fault is truly sin, which even now damns and brings eternal death to those who are not born again through Baptism and the Holy Spirit.

ONE THEOLOGIAN suggested that this is the single doctrine in Christian faith for which there is overwhelming evidence all found within the human condition! In other words, this one doctrine does not have to be argued much less proven! (Or, as Mark Twain put it: "man is the only animal that blushes. Or needs to.") One may not be able to name a television program, a movie or a popular song which does not describe "brokenness" as the human situation we call "sin." Look around: relationships are busted, motives are messed up, the world is splintered by natural and human ordered disasters, we invent new weaponry, labeled always as "defensive," subscribe to economies based on accumulation and built-in obsolescence; in short, we are all in trouble. The root of all this is sin: our separation from God; resulting in our defiant rebellion against God and God's will. Cultures often have treated the symptoms of sin and missed the mark here too: for example, once upon a time it was sinful to

6

play cards, dance, curse, drink and carouse. (May still be!) But behaviors only described symptoms; the disease itself is a condition called sin. And there is overwhelming evidence to prove this reality. Look around!

Sometimes, we will hear parents object that children are innocent and pure. I remember one psychologist on a talk show who cited an experiment with infants barely able to crawl. 10 were placed on a mat in a room, each was given one toy and adults left the room to observe. In a matter of minutes, two children collected all the toys, three seemed dis-interested, three were crying and two went to sleep! How's that for commentary on the human situation?

I was a guest preacher in a vacant congregation one Sunday and the organist said she would handle the "childrens' moment and that she had six treats because that was the number of children in the parish. On that Sunday one brought a guest so what would she do? She looked at one of the children and said to him, "since you live close to me, I'll give you a double treat tomorrow." At the same time, a woman in the congregation had a candy bar in her purse and was bringing it down the aisle to offer it and the little boy saw her coming and shouted out . . . "no, stop, I'll take double on Monday." I believe that the proofs of genetic sinfulness abound.

Among pastors, counselors and therapists, the entry of parishioner/patient into one's office with an appointment, will often mean the telling of personal stories with a variation on the theme of sin: adultery, abuse, alienation, anger, lives bent out of shape or busted up, confession, confusion, depression, despair, (this list is beginning to appear like A, B, C cataloging of common catastrophes, and so it is!) There is truth in the Gospel according to Mother Goose, "humpty dumpty sat on a wall, humpty dumpty had a great fall, all the king's horses and all the king's men, couldn't put humpty together again," so yes, there is a very real human condition and all of our wealth, power, technology and will power cannot put anything together again. Great damage is done. "Sin" is rampant and there seems to be an epidemic of it going around.

(And the "original" in "original sin" simply means that the brokenness is truly passed on via genetic generation, one birth to the next from Adam (every one) and Eve (mother of all living). So, we have great need for "Savior," the topic of Article three.

Questions for Reflection

- Many think that babies have no sin; that sin is the accumulation of "bad things done." What do you think?

- Some churches provide for a general "confession of sins" in worship liturgies. What is the value of such silent moments? Is there a place for individual confession of sins and when would one make use of such a moment?

- What does baptism have to do with the forgiveness of sins?

- If we are reconciled in Jesus Christ, how are we reconciled to one another?

ARTICLE 3

"Concerning the Son of God"

Likewise they teach that the Word, that is, the Son of God, took upon himself human nature in the womb of the blessed Virgin Mary so that there might be two natures, divine and human, inseparably conjoined in the unity of one person, one Christ, truly God and truly a human, being "born of the Virgin Mary," who truly "suffered, was crucified, died, and was buried" that he might reconcile the Father to us and be a sacrifice not only for original guilt but also for actual sins of human beings. He also "descended into hell, and on the third day he was truly "resurrected." Thereafter, "he ascended into heaven" in order to "sit at the right hand of the Father," and he will reign forever and have dominion over all creatures. He will sanctify those who believe in him by sending into their hearts the Holy Spirit, who will rule, console, and make them alive and defend them against the devil and the power of sin. The same Christ will publicly return to judge the living and the dead . . . according to the Apostles' Creed.

THE WHOLE question of the two natures of Christ (human and divine) continues to play into the life of the church in some unexpected ways. Our century sees the church, for example, waging what are called "worship wars." One way of thinking about this is to note that different peoples in different times ac-

9

cent one or the other attributes of Christ. In the epoch of great cathedral building, the transcendence of God was communicated in splendor and awe. God was "high and lifted up" and the eye was drawn heavenward to majestic, sweeping carved arches of gothic architecture. Stories were "read" in columns of stained glass and music echoed through cavernous transepts in splendid chants of wafted sound. Incense, with its clouds of smoke inside the churches, proclaimed a meeting place of heaven and earth (as well as the functional need for fumigation!). With sermon and sacraments, sights, sounds and smells, the church brought its Gospel to people through all five human senses. In such "concrete" ways of experience, the focus was on a transcendent and divine God, beyond us, and above us.

In the 19th, 20th and 21st centuries, the focus shifts to the human Jesus and the "immanence" of God among us and with us. The all time favorite popular hymn "Amazing Grace" speaks of "me" . . . "I" am the lost, the blind, the wretch; it is "I" with fears, dangers, toils and snares. And what I want is "Blessed Assurance," in all this trouble and danger. And together we proclaim "what a friend we have in Jesus." Church architecture tends to be of two types: "performing stages" where the performance of sermon and song is seen, felt, experienced and enjoyed or, "living rooms" where the people assemble to be comfortable in padded pews and celebrate an incarnational Word-in-our-midst. See how architectural choices make theological statements!

Theologian Paul Scherer once said that instead of singing "blessed assurance, Jesus is mine;" the corrective phrase would instead say, "blessed disturbance, I am his." The phrase about the Word of God being a two edged sword has two applications: to comfort the afflicted and afflict the comfortable. Likewise, the two natures of Christ are a unity. This Messiah person is both human and divine. There is both an imminent and a transcendent God. The paradox with which we live is that God is both as close to me as a best friend and yet so beyond that the "awesome wonder" combines fear and reverence in an experience of true transcendence. The Son of God as both human and divine and the ancient creeds testify to both when the Church confesses, "born of Mary, suffered, died and was buried," and "on the third day he rose." The two natures of Jesus have been focused pronouncements revealed by God.

Article three continues to speak of why this Son of God came to us. Some years ago, as many of the "baby boomers" were returning to church, a national news magazine interviewed a young woman about her homecoming to church. She said she prided herself on giving her 5 year old child the best of everything including school, sports, travel and all material goods. But one day in an art museum the Mom and daughter paused before a painting of the crucifixtion and the girl asked, "Mommy, what is that man doing up there?" She said her long absence from church had this moment as a wake-up call leading to their return. The question lingers however in Article three of the Augsburg Confession: "what is that man doing up there?" Here we see a death, freely given, that we might be forgiven, set free from sin and death, and have life bestowed. This gracious work of the death of Jesus is truly "for us and for our salvation." Only God could do this and it is pure unmerited love that shows such sacrifice for our sakes. This leads to the Gospel lens so radically focused among Lutherans in article four.

Questions for Reflection

- Who do people today say Jesus is?

- Do you find yourself holding "human and divine" together in Jesus or grasping one or the other in your thinking about him?

- How do we use the earthly life of Jesus to inform the work and deeds of the resurrected Christ among us?

- Does the architecture of your worship space speak more of the human or divine natures of Jesus?

ARTICLE 4

"Concerning Justification"

> *Likewise they teach that human beings cannot be justified before God by their own powers, merits, or works. But they are justified as a gift on account of Christ through faith when they believe that they are received into grace and that their sins are forgiven on account of Christ, who by his death made satisfaction for our sins. God reckons this faith as righteousness (Romans 3: 21–26 and 4: 5).*

EVERY SUNDAY, seated in our congregations, are persons of all ages conditioned to think, act and believe according to a nearly universally understood and accepted "work ethic." The formula simply says success is a result of hard work. We believe in a rewards/merit system. Play hard and the athlete will move upward from club to junior varsity to varsity. Report cards can be improved from C's to A's with work, dedication and perseverance. I remember the layperson who served as the "poet laureate" of Trinity Lutheran Church, Grand Rapids, Michigan, (Clem Block) who once wrote a poem entitled, "No Report Cards in Heaven," verse one: "there will be no report cards in heaven; you won't get an 'A' or a 'D'—Were you a success or a failure? Will never be asked of me." Good thought about justification! It will not be a matter of a graded sequence! Nearly everything we know is on a "ladder climb" progression: baby to toddler, child to adolescent, young adult to mature adult; elementary to middle school, high school to college; from private to general; from entry level to corporate exec.—all of these "climbs" are about a way of thinking, living and succeeding. People pull themselves up by their bootstraps. The Weber thesis entitled "the Protestant ethic and the spirit of capitalism" showcases a rewards system that has everyone convinced about how the world, business, school and life all work. And for many pieces of it all, it does! In life, there is much growth, change, experience, maturity, development and blossoming of talents, gifts and abilities and this is exactly the way the whole enterprise of communal life is ordered. Thus, there comes a radical "stop sign" to such rewards and enterprises when we come face to face with grace and it may cause a theological crash! You mean, I can't work hard and get this grace? You mean I can't earn the merit badges to attain a higher rank in the kingdom? You mean there is nothing I can do to deserve God's love and make myself worthy of God's attention? You mean my own strength, ability, finesse and power can't get me on the good side of God? There is a radical reformation commentary on this matter: our relationship, our standing with God is *nothing* we merit, earn or deserve but is purely a free gift. It echoes Paul's words in the epistle to the Romans: "we are justified by grace through faith." (Romans 3:23–26) So, what do we do to have a right relationship with God? We can do nothing! We can only *receive* grace we cannot get it. Such gifted "receiving" is anti-culture in every way since we are trained to live, act, think and believe according to a system of rewards. Report card evaluations of worth and merit are shredded in the light of grace and faith. To persons who have been stuffed into oppressive confinements about meritorious service and self-worth, the good news in this glimpse of grace is like opening a window and basking in the cool breeze of a new springtime refreshment of scented oxygen, with the delight of colorful blossoms all around and a splash of sunlight all beginning a new day! Such is the joy of this precious gift.

Besides the human penchant for merits and credits and proving ourselves, there is yet another web in which we are entangled. The Scriptures tell us that we are a "caught" people:

- caught in the things we do that we can't make right;

- caught in circumstances not of our doing;

- caught in attempts to always justify, rationalize and explain our choices and behaviors.

And yet many of have experienced what it means to be loved "in spite of" any of the entrapments which ensnare us. When the child comes running and screaming in sorrow because they break a parent's favorite treasure (something we do), or when they are sick or hurt (a circumstance we did not cause), or when they did something that turns out to be wrong, hurtful or destructive (behaviors and choices) the parent can either lower the boom and punish the offender or receive the child with an open-armed embrace. Love may show itself both in punishment or in suspension of judgment but *forgiveness* is what restores the relationship and permits a new beginning. When we receive grace-filled forgiveness, we are surprised and our self-justification is shattered. We had expected and deserved judgment but we receive mercy. This is the work, word and promise of Jesus. His life, death and resurrection freely give a relationship with God that we cannot do for ourselves. We can only receive it as a gift. This is the very heart of the good news in Christ Jesus. The three parables in St. Luke, chapter 15, illustrate the heart of God to welcome, to rejoice and to restore the lost (the lost coin, the lost sheep and the lost son). God seeks and finds. God patiently waits. But when the lost is found, when the dead is made alive, the good news makes its rounds and the celebration of reconciliation begins! What pure gift!

But next, one wonders about the receiving of such pure grace. How/where/what is this receiving? Is it randomly given to some and not to others? For the reception of such grace, God has instituted the office of ministry, subject of article five.

Questions for Reflection

- Is there such a thing as a "free lunch?"
- If the world conditions us in a system of rewards and punishments, how do we grasp God's grace?
- What are the "sneaky" ways we make grace conditional in our words and deeds?
- Are there illustrations in your own life of pure grace (a time when you expected punishment and received mercy)?

REFORMATION HISTORY ON THE ARTICLE OF JUSTIFICATION

On the occasion of the 450th anniversary of the Augsburg Confession, Dr. Eric Gritsch (op. cit., Feb. 6, 1980) wrote:

> The medieval church was the steward of life and death. People lived as members of the church which cared through words and sacraments for their welfare on earth and taught them how to die for the world to come. People feared life after death more than death itself. History discloses that humans usually regard life as dominated by credit, merit or any other if-then relationships—if you do this, then you receive that. The Judeo-Christian designation of such a relationship is "original sin." It is the drive in all human creatures to control relationships with each other and with God through if-then propositions. Adam and Eve fell because they wanted to be like God—being in charge of good and evil and living forever. . . . Luther learned and was told to practice that the way to God was through the accumulation of moral credits (good works) supplemented by the addition of spiritual infusions (sacraments). There is sufficient free will after the fall of Adam and Eve to lift oneself out of the mire of

> sins and, beginning with baptism, to add sufficient merit
> by faithfully obeying the will of the church expressed in
> the relationship between penance (the confession of sins)
> and satisfaction (the granting of forgiveness).[1]

Ultimately, for Luther, the intense personal, spiritual and biblical struggle about this relationship, "discovered the deceptively simple truth that God's righteousness is a gift received through faith rather than a wage earned through good works. He discovered that God relates to his creation like a father to his children—unconditionally accepting them without asking for merit. This kind of trusting acceptance was 'faith.'"[2] The impact of this "freeing discovery" for Luther had a further implication, as Gritsch puts it, "that the church consists of mutually trusting disciples rather than credit seeking members, and that led him into conflict with medieval ecclesiastical authority."[3]

FUTHER DISCOURSE ON JUSTIFICATION

To really "get" the gist of the importance of this article, one must grasp the Gospel's sense of "word power." The Scriptures are replete with Word power. God speaks and the creation comes into existence "out of nothing." When Jacob tricks his brother Easu out of his birthright, it is because Isaac has "spoken" (i.e., used words) for a blessing that, once out of his mouth, cannot be taken back. While modern people have some sense of "contract" as in, "read the fine print," the covenant making in biblical times had to do with "word power." When one spoke a blessing or curse or spoke a promise or covenant it was done. As a pastor, I often use this with couples bringing a child for baptism. There is the child at birth who enters this world subject to the fallen creation's reality of sin and death. Then, at the baptismal font, a word comes, "you are baptized in the Name of the Father and of the Son and

1. Gritsch, "Central Pennsylvania Synod."

2. Ibid.

3. Ibid.

of the Holy Spirit," and with water and word, this child is no longer just the parents' child, no longer a child subject to creation's falleness, but this one is newly "born from above," now to be a child of God! Such "word power," such word pronouncement is what continues to bring something out of nothing and has the character of producing that which God declares. So, if we look to our church's liturgy, there are instances where "word power" makes something just so:

- There is the invocation promising the presence of God, Father, Son and Holy Spirit, now to be with us as we assemble.

- There is the absolution, when the pastor proclaims that by the grace of Christ, our sin is forgiven, and it is! The Word of God makes it so.

- There are the words "this is my body given for you; this is my blood given and shed for you for the forgiveness of sin" and, it is so.

- When, at the liturgy's conclusion, we are sent out with the benediction, we depart with the very blessing of God given to us for this is the "Word power" of God to make it so. Therefore, when forgiveness of sin is announced by God's representative (usually an ordained minister called and set apart to do this), the very pronouncement is valid for it rests on God's promise alone. This is Word-power: promise-announcing and covenant-making; this is God delivering a wondrous thing! Such Word power takes flesh in a baby's birth in Bethlehem, turns water into wine, casts out demons, stills a storm, causes the blind to see and the dead to live. We trust the Word power of God. "Justification" is about that kind of power to forgive and restore a relationship. Forgiveness is real for it comes to us as a free gift and rests on the promise and covenant of God's Word alone. Trust this to be so!

Article 5

"Concerning Ministry in the Church"

> *So that we may obtain this faith, the ministry of teaching the Gospel and administering the sacraments was instituted. For through the Word and the sacraments, as through instruments, the Holy Spirit is given, who effects faith, where and when it pleases God in those who hear the gospel, that is to say, in those who hear that God, not on account of our own merits but on account of Christ justifies those who believe that they are received into grace on account of Christ. Gal. 3:14, "So that we might receive the promise of the Spirit through faith . . ."*

THE WORD and the Sacraments are the means through which our God gives the Spirit who works faith. Are we surprised that God would use such "material" sensory "stuff" as a way of getting through to us? If God is Spirit and Spirit is invisible and goes where it wills, and there are spiritual feelings and experiences, how can we speak of God and things of the Spirit attaching to such ordinary stuff as our words, our water, our bread and wine? Consider: God brought the "stuff" into existence, all of it, and called it good! God spoke Word of life in call (i.e., Abraham and Moses and others) and confrontation and admonition (i.e., prophets) and in guidance and boundaries (i.e., ten commandments). And then, in the fullness of time, God becomes a baby in a manger; in the life story of Jesus, God works wonders, speaks life and finally suffers, dies and is buried. During the sweep of his Gospel, he commands his followers to "go and baptize and teach" and at his last supper he takes the bread and wine and says "do this." These actions and items were not "mimed" or pantomimed; they are not ideas left to our imagination, they are gifts to the Church to take and "taste and see that the Lord is good." We do these things *as instructed*. The commands are validated when Jesus is raised from the dead and has us remember these "means" to continue a future opening grace through forgiveness of sin and new life. For the express communication of the Gospel and promissory Word attached to the earthly elements, God instituted an "office" within the people of God to see to these things. The ministerial office is one to which persons are called; these called ones undertake a stewardship of the treasured Gospel vowing to faithfully teach/preach, transmit, embody and enact its trajectories wherever and however they lead. Churches have organized in a plethora of ways over the centuries. There is some consensus historically that has been built around a three-fold office of bishop, presbyter (pastor) and deacon. Others have maintained the pastoral office alone as the focus of such ministry while still others use the New Testament epistle listings of apostles, prophets, teachers, healers, helpers, evangelists, administrators, etc. as the roles within the office.

In *Christian Century Magazine* (March 7, 2005), Gordon Atkinson wrote:

> (he talks about what he thought of preachers . . . he didn't know where they came from or where they went when they were finished. He says he thought of them as either givers of sacred knowledge or persons of inspirational character; then he says . . .)
>
> "Sometimes it was hard to think of the preacher as a person at all. He was just a part of the architecture of the place, just a piece of the church. To do church properly,

one needs a steeple, a bell perhaps, some hymnals, some pews, a preacher, a pulpit, a few candles and so on.

Sometimes I thought about the preacher, but mostly not. Mostly I just sat in the pew and watched the words fall upon the congregation like fertilizer on the lawn. The words fell on our heads and settled into our midst, ending up on the pews and on the floor. On a good day something might get under your skin or into your heart.

And now I'm one of those preachers, I'm up front looking out at you, looking out at rows and rows of faces. And though I have taken this mysterious journey myself, I still can't tell you how a person becomes a preacher."[1]

One of the great assurances in this article is the insistence that God has instituted an office and this office does not belong to us. We did not make it; we cannot sustain it. It is larger than any of us and our individual personalities. It is an office: a public office. Through this office the Gospel truly gets taught and preached from surprising places. A well known theologian told a story to a group of pastors about a time in his "first call" parish, when he had to speak to a close friend and parishioner family about the impending death of the father/husband. They asked him to be the one to tell the six year old son. He began by saying that he said to the boy, "you know your Dad is really, really sick," and he said this to think a six year old could comprehend that the next thing would be death. But the little boy simply said, "yes, I know he's sick." Then the pastor had to speak the words, "we know he is going to die." And the child cried. The pastor knew that it was his time to speak but he could not. So in the sobbing, the little boy looks up and says, "When he dies, I know he will go to heaven." "I know that Jesus will raise him up some day but that's a long time to wait." The pastor recalls that on that day, the child spoke the Gospel, not the pastor. The pastor, in his own silent grief, heard

---

1. Atkinson, "Said the Cowboy to His People."

from the child. The point is that God will get the Gospel spoken; it may not always be the ordained, but it will get spoken. *"And a little child shall lead them."* How thankful we are to God for instituting a ways and means to convey good news.

Finally, Martin Luther writes a wonderful description of the work of a pastor when he is appealing to the German princes to support such pastoral work.

He says:

> . . . to support or protect a poor, pious pastor is an act that makes no show and looks like a small thing. But to build a marble church, to give it golden ornaments, and to serve dead stone and wood—that makes a show that glitters! That is a virtue worthy of a king or prince! Well, let it make its show! Let it glitter! Meanwhile, my pastor, who does not glitter, is practicing the virtue that increases God's kingdom, fills the heaven with saints, plunders hell, robs the devil, wards off death, represses sin, instructs and comforts every person in the world according to his station in life, preserves peace and unity, raises fine young folk and plants all kinds of virtue in the people. In a word, he is making a whole new world! He builds not a poor temporary house, but an eternal and beautiful Paradise, in which God is glad to dwell. A pious prince or lord who supports or protects such a pastor can have a part in all this.[2]

How's that for a pastoral job description? But this is the Gospel's truth and the Gospel's work through the public office of ministry! And here is the confidence of this article: that the Holy Spirit, through the Word and the Sacraments, produces faith where and when it pleases God in those who hear the Gospel. Such faith leads to a radical new obedience, Article six.

2. Luther, *Luther's Works*, 52–53.

Questions for Reflection

- Is there a difference between jobs and "calls?"

- What particular responsibilities are charged to the office of pastor, i.e., what does "ordination" mean or do?

- Can and when would a lay person take up the responsibilities of Word and Sacrament?

- Where do pastors come from and how is such a call nurtured?

Article 6

"Concerning the New Obedience"

Likewise, they teach that this faith is bound to yield good fruits and that it ought to do good works commanded by God on account of God's will and not so that we may trust in these works to merit justification before God. For forgiveness of sins, and justification are taken hold of by faith, as the saying of Christ also testifies, (Luke 17:10): "when you have done all things, say, 'we are worthless slaves.'" The authors of the ancient church teach the same. For Ambrose says, "It is established by God that whoever believes in Christ shall be saved, without work by faith alone, receiving the forgiveness of sins as a gift."

THERE IS no way to measure the *faith* of a person or of a congregation. But there are various ways to measure the *good works* of persons and congregations and our congregations do excel in good works! Across the whole of Christendom, it is difficult to even imagine our world without the influence of Christian faith that has poured itself into the betterment of humankind. The Church has brought forth schools, colleges and universities, hospitals, nursing homes, retirement villages, hunger appeals, global missions, food banks, shelter programs, clothing exchanges, disaster response, visitation of the sick, grieving and imprisoned, acts of kindness and charity by multi-millions of people through centuries of time. And individual stories abound and the creativity of parishioners is wondrous in the gifts and offerings of the very good works of God's faithful.

She was an elderly parishioner newly confined to wheelchair and bed. After initial questions of "why me?" she thought what could be made of her situation. I remember the afternoon conversation . . . "pastor, I'm not much good for anything. But I just figured out that I am good on the phone. I'd like to call shut-ins on behalf of the church and just speak to some people each day." When this offer got underway, she hardly ever again thought of herself as shut-in or confined. Her bedroom became "traffic control central" for the congregation. She would listen to people and give them encouragement; she would give us a prayer list for the coming Sunday; she would hear of a special need and relay it to the church office. She truly took her limitations and discovered a new calling for her life. What a gift!

One of the children in our congregation entered a poster contest sponsored by one of the church's social ministry agencies. When he was rewarded with the $50. first prize, he told his mother he wanted to 'tiith" (tithe) his money. She had no idea he knew the word "tithe" much less what it meant. When he gave his $5.00 offering, I wished that the more adult members could emulate the "little child who leads them." I did find ways to illustrate his generosity as an expression of offering!

Another elderly woman in one parish said she had once been a visitor to a congregation and received a hand written note from the pastor instead of a typed letter. That so impressed her that she gave Monday morning to sending those notes with the pastor's signature (I often wondered if any visitor later would compare my handwriting to hers).

One of the church's most explosive mandates is pronounced at the end of liturgy and the beginning of service: "go in peace, serve the Lord!" Such diakonia, serving, is integral to the mission of the church. Whether one refers to such acts as good deeds or "fruits of the spirit" or results of our "new obedience," the good acts of God's people, impact and flavor the whole world. Here, there is a two-track propulsion: the individual Christian's good deeds, and the deeds of a faithful community, the church. Wherever we work with integrity and goodness and excellence, the Gospel is given witness. When we do "the right thing," God rejoices. When we advocate for the poor, the oppressed, the marginalized, God says "well done." There would be millions upon millions of individual "profiles in courage" if the story of Christendom's good deeds could be told.

Likewise, the story of congregational life is replete with instances of service in ways that make a huge difference in peoples' lives. The habitat and shelter projects, the soup kitchens and food pantries, the building of schools, hospitals, nursing homes and ancillary agencies is amazing. The multi-millions of dollars in food and medicine, education and care-taking speak of the church's generous and good heart. Annually, the budget of a congregation is an annual theological document directing the congregation's will into ministry and mission. And beyond the "back yard" caretaking each congregation is about, there is a whole global world of opportunities to give. The Christian Church has had this self-understanding that since our "God so loved the world, that God gave. . . ," so too, shall God's people. Also, the New Testament epistles lift up great examples of congregations giving both out of their poverty or from their abundance for the needs of others. Such good deeds are wonderful not as exercises in obtaining salvation or enhancing our standing before God, but as a response to the great grace God has poured forth to us in Jesus Christ. Yes, every Christian is the doer of good deeds!

Questions for Reflection

- What "good deeds" from other people, come to mind in your personal biography? In your congregation?

- Have you considered the liturgical dismissal, "go in peace, serve the Lord," to be a commission each week to places where you spend your time?

- Name some of your congregation's collective witness in serving.

- Do good deeds become a way of life or remain a constant struggle?

Article 7

"Concerning the Church"

Likewise they teach that one holy church will remain forever. The church is the assembly of saints in which the gospel is taught purely and the sacraments are administered rightly. And it is enough for the true unity of the church to agree concerning the teaching of the gospel and the administration of the sacraments. It is not necessary that human traditions, rites and ceremonies, instituted by human beings, should be alike everywhere. As Paul says (Eph. 4: 5,6), "One faith, one baptism, one God and Father of all . . ."

I USED to tell our confirmands that one particular wrong answer would jeopardize their confirmation: if I asked them, "what is the church?" and they answered, "a building," they were in trouble! One of their earliest Sunday school songs taught them correctly, "I am the church, you are the church, we are church together." How the meeting places differ around the world and perhaps you have seen this too: assemblies gather in great and grand cathedrals, camp amphitheaters around campfires, lodge halls, grass huts, storefronts, living rooms, school cafeterias, bowling alleys, trailers; in hotel ballrooms and under outdoor tent tarps; also, in stadiums and domed wonders of the world! In these places we find "church." I still like my theologian teacher, Robert Jenson's, explanation: "the church is whoever shows up."

When an assembly gathers in the Name of Jesus and around the Word, the bath and the meal, there we find the church.

If one could unravel the DNA of the Church, one would discover what is exactly proposed in this article: the Word of God and the sacraments of God are constitutive of "church." God has set in motion a way of getting to us, a way of getting through to us. If we wonder about the "mysteries" of God and if there is "transcendence" to a God who is obviously beyond us humans, then the means of God getting through is a huge comfort to every one of us. Therefore, there is the Word of God contained in the human words of Gospel preachers. There is a gift of grace packaged in the water and bread and wine to be outpoured upon us, handed to us, so that a word and a gift are pressed into our ears, our eyes, our hands, our taste, touch, smell, all the receptors that we can use to "get" and to receive the God who comes to us and is not far off and removed.

Just as Christ has two natures, human and divine, so too does the church. The church is corpus mixtum (a mixed body). It is an assembly of "wheat and tares" growing in the kingdom field until the end. This article reminds us that that the true church continues forever. Is that a bold statement? In many of the Scandinavian churches, the altar area has a semi-circular kneeling rail. In teaching about this architectural novelty, it is understood that the church of earth, kneeling here, is the church visible but that the church invisible (in heaven) completes the circle. This is a wonderful image. Calvin's words about this are helpful, "the chief end of any person is to praise God and enjoy God forever!" So, the church's worship on earth and the church's worship in heaven will be an eternal choir of praise and worship forever. (I particularly enjoy this thought when looking out on a congregation where one sees persons holding hymnals without singing and acting disengaged from the worship. Won't they be surprised some day?)

But the child whines, "why do I have to go to church?" Our parental answer was always, "because Jesus expects us to." God insisted that a day of worship be maintained; it was called Sabbath rest. Jesus said, "where two or three gather in my Name, there I am in their midst." In the Lord's mandate to "baptize and teach," a body is formed (the church) and the body comes to gather (and together) around word, bath and meal (the assembly of saints).

Finally, in this article, there is the matter of church unity. If the great schism of the church once divided east and west, and if the Reformation further splintered the church, our last century has certainly witnessed attempts to heal the breach. Earlier ecumenical attempts often spoke of organizational mergers as a goal of unity. Without merging, indeed, while maintaining particular denominational identities, the great discovery in recent times has been in the phrase "communio," a moving from interim communion to full communion. When dialogues and long relationships show that the Gospel is taught and preached "purely" and the sacraments are administered "rightly," institutional mergers do not have to be the goal, but full acknowledgement of the validity of other church's teachings and practices is. This step gives possibilities to new and varied relationships into a promising future.

Questions for Reflection

- What does God/Father/Son and Holy Spirit have to do with "church?'

- What does "pure" Gospel taught and sacraments administered "rightly" mean?

- How do you respond to someone who says "you can be a good Christian without the church?

- In your congregation, what are some of the local signs of churches striving for unity?

ARTICLE 8

"What Is the Church?"

Although the church is properly speaking, the assembly of saints and those who truly believe, nevertheless, because in this life many hypocrites and evil people are mixed in with them, a person may use the sacraments even whey they are administered by evil people. This accords with the saying of Christ, (Matt. 23: 2): "the scribes and Pharisees sit on Moses' seat . . . " Both the sacraments and the Word are efficacious because of the ordinance and command of Christ even when offered by evil people.

A WRITER in *Partners Magazine* carried one of my favorite columns by Pastor Steve McKinley. He describes a late night phone call from an anonymous person he calls "Lisa."

"Lisa, do I know you, are you a member of this congregation?" "No, you don't know me. I don't belong to any church. Churches are so full of hypocrites, you know." (I bit my tongue to keep from giving one or both responses to that which came immediately to mind. Option A: Really? I had *no* idea that there were hypocrites in the church," or, Option B: Always room for one more.") "The institutional church is such a turn-off for me," she continued. "Organized religion is dull. But I consider myself a very religious person. I'm quite spiritual. I watch Dr. 'so and so" every Sunday. I think of him

as my pastor." (I had another response ready for that: "if
you think of him as your pastor, why don't you give old
Dr. 'so and so' a call?")[1]

"Hypocrite" comes from the Greek for stage actor. It is one
who merely plays a part. Obviously, the church is full of such
ones including you, me and all the rest of the gang. The chasm
between what we say and what we do is huge. Of course, we wish
for the integrity of wholeness; we wish we could be combina-
tions of pure motives and self-less actions. We shall have to wait
on the parousia for that! So, in the meantime, we have who we
are and what we are. And this is legitimately a turn-off for many
or at least a reason to stay away from church. Mark Twain said,
"I would not want to belong to any organization that would have
me for a member!" Sorry, Samuel Clemens (two names?), the
church is just graceful enough to have you anyway! But obviously if anything depended on me or my integrity or motivation, all
would soon implode and collapse due to our hypocrisy. So, this
articles speaks so directly, "both the sacraments and the Word
are efficacious by reason of the institution and commandment of
Christ." Thank God!

When a young couple would come to me to prepare for
marriage, we would spend one conversation on the subject of
covenants: how our words and promises would cause a new thing
(marriage) to come into being. I called this the moment of the "holy
chill." It's that moment we you arrive at the chancel of a church as
two single individuals. Then some words are spoken by each in
the form of a promise and the two depart as a married couple.
Everyone who has heard the words, knows that a new relationship
has come into being. The rings will be the visible, outward sign of
the words spoken. If our words have such power, how much more
does God's word have power! God speaks and creation comes out
of nothing! And I go on to talk about the power of God's Word in

1. McKinley, "Pastor Loci."

four places in the liturgy: the absolution in which God forgives sin, "through Christ, you are forgiven . . ."

In Holy Baptism, "I baptize you in the Name of the Father and of the Son and of the Holy Spirit," now you are a child of God. Before this powerful Word was spoken, you were a child of creation but not of kingdom; after the Word, you are. "This is my body, my blood, given for you for the forgiveness of sin." And it is so! "The Lord bless you and keep you." In absolution, baptism, holy communion and benediction, the mighty Word of God calls into being something that was not before the speaking, before the promise making took place. That is powerful Word of creation, of covenant and of communion! When wedding vows are exchanged, it is one of the few moments when we might experience what it is to speak some words, promissory in nature, and have a new thing come into existence. This, God does all the time!

A story is told of Napoleon passing by on his horse in reviewing a line of military 'privates.' Suddenly, the horse bolted and one soldier jumped from the line to grab the reigns and Napoleon said, "why thank you captain!" "Of what regiment sir?" he answered. The field promotion was immediately grasped by the foot soldier. The emperor's all powerful word had the capacity to bestow an elevated rank . . . on the spot. And one believed it immediately. Another military person in a New Testament story (called a 'centurion') once had a daughter who was seriously ill, near death. When he approached Jesus about her situation, Jesus was ready to go to her but the soldier said, "Just speak the Word and she will be healed," (John 4: 46–53). Just speak the Word. What a testimony to faith and belief.

We hypocrites, *thank God* that the promise making we speak relies not on us, but on God. What we declare does not depend on our delivery of what is promised but everything relies and depends on God. We spokespersons are full of it! "It" meaning sin and death, hypocrisy and mixed motives, but we are vessels for declaration; mouth pieces for proclamation. While we were yet sinners, we dared to speak a Word not our own, but of God and then to trust that God chooses such "clay pots" to be containers of precious treasure. Such are the ways of God.

Questions for Reflection

- Sometimes, "sincerity" is one of our highest values. Does this article of faith free us from such dependency? Why or why not?

- What personal illustrations can you think of when words were life-changing for you?

- How does the church deal with the issue of hypocrisy used by some to stay away from faith?

- Do you expect ministry leaders to be exemplars of faith?

"Concerning Baptism"

> *Concerning baptism they teach that it is necessary*
> *for salvation, that the grace of God is offered through*
> *baptism, and that children should be baptized. They*
> *are received into the grace of God when they are of-*
> *fered to God through baptism.*

Pastors never forget some of the settings of especially memorable baptisms. I remember the "middle of the night" call with a father frantically talking about pre-mature labor and the baby might die. The 3 A.M. walk into a hospital PICU is a heavy walk. The parents are in a separate room in a time of shock and numb disbelief. The question of the baby's survival is pondered between gushing tears and dry heaves of sad fright. But they are clear about one thing, "Pastor can you go in an baptize our baby?" The nurses and staff are prepared for that. Even their heavy hearts agree with this urgent act of comfort and hope. They whisper some instructions, dress you in gown and mask and lead the parents in a silent processional. There is no crucifer, no pipe organ accompaniment and no mighty chorus of singers this day, just a quiet entourage of a faithful few entering a different kind of holy place and holy space. The incubator box is the new necessary womb. One wonders if it is a cubicle for life or a casket for death. A small sterile bottle of water with an eyedropper has been placed inside where your gloved hands can reach and apply the water and you choke with the words you speak, "I baptize you in the Name of the Father and of the Son and of the Holy Spirit." Prayers are spoken, benediction is pronounced and a silent vigil begins. The Mom needs rest and a silent recessional takes you back to the room. This has been a scenario twice in my pastoral ministry. In both PICU cases, the babies lived! Later, in their first Sunday in worship, they were brought forward with the liturgical celebration from the occasional services for "public recognition" of baptism. Some of the story was told about their perilous entry into the world; the act of baptism in the incubator setting and thanksgiving for the life now among us.

Other hospital journeys have not had the happy endings. I particularly remember two miscarriages and the great sadness of death with the parents in those hospital settings. Both asked if a baptism could be done. (Theologically, church teaching does not allow for such a sacrament for the dead but the instincts of pastoral care devise others ways of approaching this for the proclamation of the Gospel and the comfort of the parents). A phrase such as: "we now entrust this child to the arms of Jesus and lift you to him in the Name of the Father and of the Son and of the Holy Spirit," gives the Name of the Triune God as comfort in a prayerful way to the parents. Are there other options of speaking? One might use a bit of water with the sign of the cross saying, "holy child, if we had been graced with your life among us, we would have entrusted you to the same God to whom we now turn, in the Name of the Father and of the Son and of the Holy Spirit." In both instances of life and death, the parents turn to the Church for the good Word of a promise from God. Every wonderful impulse is to turn for assurance to the grace of God in Christ Jesus: *grace* in the waters of baptism, *grace* in the Name of the Triune God, *grace* in the company of the people of God so represented by the presence of the pastor. Persons in ministry need to reflect on these things and consider the whole matter of what traditionally has been called "God's pre-venient grace."

Before we ask, God knows. Before we act, God acts. Grace comes before we ask or seek. There is such comfort in this assurance.

In the case of an elderly man, his son (my parishioner) asked if his father, from out of town, could speak with me after a terminal prognosis had been spoken to him. In the conversation, the man had supported his wife and family with their church involvements through the years. He had been an attender of a congregation but had not revealed a rather guarded secret, he had never been baptized. His parents never went to church. His wife never asked the question, he just went along to church with the children in tow all those years. Everyone thought he had been a baptized member for years. Some of the "secret" had to do with his thoughts of not being worthy; some had to do with the embarrassment of having a guarded secret for years and then pastors had come and gone in the congregation with assumptions being made all along. The thought of having only a few days to live brought this conversation to a new urgency. Might he be baptized in the hospital bed? The font was a plastic wash tub, the congregation was family members. He felt that the faith he had known now needed the outward "sign" for completion. Now would his new birth day be a death day as well? The words of the funeral liturgy seemed to know the man and the circumstances: "when we were baptized in Christ Jesus, we were baptized into his death . . . for if we have been united with him in a death like his, we shall certainly be united with him in a resurrection like his."

Pastors also know the "absurdities" that surround baptism when parents just want to get the kid "done." One family visited the church for a couple of weeks and then asked about baptizing their baby. The conversation took a turn when the parents asked that the setting be in a hotel banquet hall booked by the parents for a family reunion just three weeks hence. I spoke of the congregation and its worship as the setting for baptism except in emergency circumstances. Incredibly, in a round of golf the next week, my colleague, the Presbyterian pastor, revealed this same story about a couple who came shopping for a baptismal officiant! In a tribute to ecclesial unity, we had both given the same response to the parents!

Parents, sponsors and the congregation gather round to make promises to raise the newly baptized in the faith of the church. Promises are made to "bring to the services of God's house, teach them the 10 commandments, the Lord's prayer and the creed, place in their hands the Scriptures and see to their instruction in the Christian faith." When these vows are kept, there is wonderful unfolding of a faith adventure in the lives of children, parents and sponsors and, when the vows are discarded or ignored, how the hearts of many are pained. It is a glorious moment to behold the times when the wish and hopes of parents truly correspond to the will of God! Baptism is one such moment. Yet often, baptismal grace continues to be a trail of a persistent God-story when the "hound of heaven" stays in pursuit of God's children by water and the Word. Such grace abounds.

Questions for Reflection

- Consider your own baptismal story. What does it mean to you?

- What might a congregation do to help strengthen the vows of parents and sponsors?

- Have you seen other church's baptisms and how do they differ and how are they alike?

- The basis for sacramental baptism of infants is that God is the initiator of the act; for those who insist on "believer's baptism," the individual is supposed to truly repent and believe and therefore be the initiator. How do you discuss the differences among your acquaintances?

ARTICLE 10

"Concerning the Supper of the Lord"

*Concerning the Lord's Supper they teach that the
body and blood of Christ are truly present and are
distributed to those who eat the Lord's Supper.*

IN MICHIGAN, our congregation was a host site for a newly
elected Bishop in the E.L.C.A. The communion distribution
used a pouring chalice and as parishioners came forward and
drank the wine, they deposited the glasses in a wicker basket.
By the end of the crowded worship, many of the small glasses
had leaked over the floor and needed to be wiped clean. One of
the ecumenical observer guests in the front pew was an official
from an Orthodox church. My elementary aged children were
fascinated by the hat he wore and went to talk with him after
worship. He talked to them about his church and then, as he
watched wine being cleaned up after the worship, he told them
that if he had spilled any in a communion service, they were
required to dig up the stone floor, replace it and have a special
blessing. So, later in the evening, the children asked their pastor/
father, "why daddy? Why must he do that?" And so the questions about Holy Communion come from different times and
places! Whether the "fear and trembling" come from a teaching
about spillage or whether it is a Martin Luther officiating at his
first Mass and breaking into a cold sweat with the thought of a
sacrificial offering of Christ to God on a German altar that he
was about to undertake, the theology and teaching about Holy

38

Communion, the elements, and the relationship of bread and wine to body and blood have shadowed the church for centuries. Across Christendom's spectrum, churches are generally divided into three understandings: those who affirm the "real presence" of Christ, those who consider it a "spiritual" event and those who understand it simply as a "memorial" re-enactment. The first group includes Roman, Orthodox, Lutheran, Anglican and Calvinists. The second group might include some Calvinists and others. The last group include Zwinglian, Anabaptists and many in the "free church" tradition (especially prevalent in the U.S.). And within each of these traditions, there are more detailed, precise theologies at work. "Real Presence" is grounded in the theological framework of a Resurrected, living Christ. The same Jesus who instituted the meal in the upper room at a last supper with his disciples, proclaimed that this, "his body and blood" is given for the forgiveness of sin. Such churches understand that this same Jesus, now risen and alive, is hosting and serving and communicating this gift *in the* present when we take, eat and drink. Many of the resurrection stories in the New Testament have a "meal presence" of the risen Jesus in which people encounter him. Especially foundational is St. Luke's story of the persons "on the road to Emmaus (Luke 24: 13–35)."

Churches with a "spiritualist" interpretation will speak of Christ being spiritually present but the risen, ascended Lord's body is in heaven and he can be with us only "spiritually."

Other "memorial" churches will not speak of real presence since it really seems to defy all human logic. All we can do is remember; think and consider Jesus, long ago, in the upper room, and in re-enacting the meal, we "think/reflect/consider" Jesus and his teachings and actions and, thus one may appropriate some values and lessons and understandings of what he was about. As a student at the College of William and Mary, Williamsburg, Virginia, I was employed as a tour guide at Jamestown Festival Park with costumes from the era of 1607. Tourists used to love the re-enactment moments of forming the guard, hearing commands, marching around the fort and illustrating how it was "back then." Memorial theology finds its value in re-enactment: some things are learned, some information is given, a scene is re-presented.

At the time of the Reformation, Luther struggled in two directions with this Eucharistic controversy. On the right, the Roman Catholics had the sacrament tied to the church and its institutional hierarchy. The church (defined as Roman) through its priests alone, via the power of ordination, only they could offer the Mass. On the left, Luther spoke with other fellow protestants at the Marburg Colloquy in 1529 in trying to resolve the difference with Zwingli and others, finally stormed out of the meeting having written with a piece of chalk on a table "hoc est meus corpus" (latin for "this is my body"). So where did Luther posit the elements of Holy Communion in this debate? Answer: on the Word alone! In the giving of bread and wine to each communicant, it is Christ's word that goes with the gift: "this is my body, this is my blood" given to you for the forgiveness of sin. This Word of a risen, living Christ effects exactly what it promises: the bread is his body, the wine is the blood of this Savior who bestows forgiveness, life and salvation to the communicant. Neither physics nor philosophy nor individual believing needs to underpin a theological system but the Word of Jesus alone is everything. A communicant's posture is simply one of trustful, humble believing/receiving/grasping of the promise of Jesus. His promises are "real" because only a living person can make promises and effect a new, open future. Dead persons can only bequeath a last will and testament (and that may be future opening in terms of resources) but someone dead may not accompany into the future (which is why resurrection is so crucial!).

The longer a pastor serves in a congregation, the more familiar one becomes with the stories/biographies, joys/sorrows as communicants come to the table of the Lord. People carry the burdens of griefs and losses, struggles in relationships and vocations and the stresses of time and pressure and yet, this "line up" of the saints/sinners coming to the table of the Lord, is a graceful parade of those hoping for a "foretaste of the feast to come."

Christmas eve worship is a wonderful celebration that the incarnate God who comes in a vulnerable baby born to peasant parents and placed in a feedbox, continues to become incarnate for us in bread and wine as we sing "Joy to the World, the Lord is Come!"

At Easter worship, the trumpets blast out that "Jesus Christ is Risen Today," and the resurrected one meets us in word and sacrament and packed congregations sing praises in exultant songs. And in between, we are fed often at our Lord's Table. In a hospital bed, a pastor raises the oxygen mask to touch a sliver of a wafer soaked in wine to a dying person's lips and the words give assurance of Jesus' accompaniment in the pass-over from death to life. A small child reaches out to the server to ask for "Jesus bread," and there is a feeding with forgiveness, life and salvation for the youngest among the worshippers. In camp settings around campfires, in prisons among the convicted, beneath tree shade in African villages, in cathedrals, churches and other places of worship, the faithful take and eat, take and drink and the mandate of Jesus to "do this," is obediently practiced and believed. We take Jesus at his word.

Questions for Reflection

- When did you first commune and can you remember what it meant for you?
- Can you describe in your own words what "real presence" of Jesus in the sacrament means?
- In recent church history, denominations have moved from "interim eucharistic fellowship" to "full communion" agreements. Have you followed any of this progres-

sion and what difference might it make in the lives of congregations and parishioners?

- Does a child with little understanding receive the benefits of this sacrament? How about an unbeliever? What is most crucial in your answer?

"Concerning Confession"

> *Concerning confession they teach that private abso-*
> *lution should be retained in the churches, although*
> *an enumeration of all faults is not necessary. For this*
> *is impossible according to the Psalm (19:12): "who*
> *can detect their errors?"*

THE WHOLE theme of confession has a biographical note of importance for me personally. In 1968 and I was a pre-law student at the College of William and Mary, Williamsburg, Virginia. I have a law professor advisor who must sign off on my courses each semester. The college has just taken religion courses out of the philosophy department and made it a separate department and there is a course I want to take called "Contemporary Christian Theology." The professor looks at my course card and asks, "why would you want to waste your time with a religion course? You must be churched or something." "Yes," I answer. "Which one?" he asks. "Lutheran," I say. "Oh, I don't like Lutherans; they do that 'confession' thing at the beginning of worship and it deflates the noble human spirit," he answers. And then a one hour conversation ensues; it has the character of a debate about confession, what is it, why would one do it, is it really necessary and on and on. I was 19 years old and in a debate with a 60 year old law school professor. Finally, he relented, "I guess you want me to sign this?" "Yes, please, if you do, I'm out of here." And so it happened. And I was "out of there" in more ways than one . . . soon, a complete turn of vocation, based on that course, from law to religion! The question lingers though: if this one man thought "confession" deflated the noble human spirit, what do others say and think about confession?

As we enter into worship, this pause and acknowledgement holds before us a mirror in which we see and own up to the reality of our human condition: we are broken, we are a mess. St. Paul's words echo a reality that even the best of counselor/therapists cannot improve upon: "the good things I would do, I don't; and the terrible things I would not do, that's what I do, so what a wretched person I am." This is the unvarnished truth about ourselves, our lives and our world. We speak it and acknowledge it and fall before God with this truth-telling. And there, in the dust and ashes of confession, we have nothing to commend ourselves and our situations to God. In this "nothingness" God speaks and proclaims good news: "arise child, your sins are forgiven not because of anything you have done to make it all right, but because Jesus offers himself on your behalf, pleads your case and now forgives you and makes you new and gives you a whole new beginning to your life NOW! And we say "WOW" and set out again like a new born baby to go play some new adventure in the world.

Still, at the time of the Reformation, many wished to do away with confession; some saw it as a ploy again for a hierarchical church to insert itself into the lives of parishioners as a way of control. There had developed a whole set of rules and regulations in which, after confession, the priest could prescribe what was necessary to make things right. The reformation commentary would be that "we cannot by our own strength or reason" or by our own will, make things right. The "making right" is a gift of God's grace. So, quickly behind this trust again in Christ alone, came some impetus to do away with confession. Thus, this article in the Augsburg confession had two foci: an endorsement again of confession as a worthy practice on the part of believers and further, that private confession/absolution would continue in the churches called "Lutheran."

While the allowance for individual confession and absolution has been retained in Lutheran churches, the only recent introduction of a liturgy form was produced in the 1978 Lutheran Book of Worship. Since congregations, for many generations, had been trained in a general confession and absolution as preparatory for Sunday worship, many parishioners began to ask where does this "individual confession" idea come from? The answer, "our Augsburg Confession." The conversation of pastor and parishioner is a very special exercise in pastoral care. There are also different orders for confession including a service of "corporate confession" and forgiveness which suggests that persons may come forward to kneel and receive an individual absolution in a personal word from the officiant. This has proved meaningful especially during Lenten worship. Still, in my experience the leap into reclaiming the service of individual confession and absolution has *not* been overwhelming. But in those instances where parishioners have come in to the office to speak of hard and difficult life situations, the use of this order to conclude the conversations has spoken powerfully to the individual in ways that other words cannot. In addition to the normal accoutrements of a pastor's office (crosses, candles, stoles/robes and home communion elements) a box of tissue is most often a sign of the sobbing conversations that pour out a life story in a stream of confession. The Roman Catholic use of confessional booths is quite common while Protestants have let such practices disappear into either general confession preparing for worship or, total absence in the disciplines of church life. Such scarcity of attention diminishes the church and the life of each Christian. Another great chasm between Roman and protestant practice is found in the manner of the "absolving" word. The Roman tradition ties confession to a number of "things to do to make things right" which is a precise criticism of the "works righteousness" accent which led to the Reformation. The absolution is meant to be a total, radical unconditional announcement and assurance that our sin is forgiven through the work and promise of Jesus Christ alone, that powerful Word and not through what we do or do not do.

Within Protestantism in general and Lutheranism in particular, the contemporary preference to omit general confession and absolution is disturbing. The good news of God in Christ Jesus is about forgiveness of sin and to find many pastors and congregations omitting this is just too much a nod to the "power of positive thinking" at the expense of "telling the truth, the whole truth and nothing but the truth" about our human condition. The reality mirror held before us is not about "deflating the noble human spirit," rather, it is about assessing the reality grasp of who we are and what we do and, in that despair, comes the very good news that we are not left in these life messes to fiend for ourselves! Christ's word of forgiveness means new life now!

Questions for Reflection

- How would you explain what is going on in "confession and absolution?"

- If any Christian can hear the confession of brother or sister, what is the role of "pastor" in such a matter?

- Are you aware of the order for "individual confession and forgiveness" and would there be a time when you would wish to make use of it?

- What is the most frequent form of confession within a family circle?

"Concerning Repentance"

Concerning repentance they teach that those who have fallen after baptism can receive forgiveness of sins whenever they are brought to repentance and that the church should impart absolution to those who return to repentance. Now, properly speaking, repentance consists of two parts: one is contrition or the terrors that strike the conscience when sin is recognized; the other is faith, which is brought to life by the gospel or absolution. This faith believes that sins are forgiven on account of Christ, consoles the conscience, and liberates it from terrors. Thereupon good works, which are the fruit of repentance, should follow.

T wo parts: contrition and absolution! And yet how difficult it is for any person to walk out of worship, having heard a word of 'absolution,' and re-enter life as a "new-born-popped-on-the-bottom-to-breathe-and-begin-life-again-all-set-free-and-made-new" person! I don't think I will ever forget a certain day in training in *clinical pastoral education* one summer day toward the end of the Vietnam War. A young woman had entered the hospital as a result of a terrible automobile accident. Her military husband was stationed overseas. The car accident involved her and a boy friend. She carried a fetus (not her husband's) and had now miscarried because of the accident. In the extreme shame of her situation, her family had totally abandoned her due to this admission of adultery and pregnancy. One person continued to come to see her: her mother. After seven days in the hospital, her mother left late one night after visiting and was killed in an auto crash. The remaining family, already judgmental and cold, now threw every accusation and blame at her. I was called in as 23 year old seminarian who listened to the sobbing grief and inconsolable guilt of this young woman. There are those times when our sighs are too deep for words and then the Holy Spirit intercedes for us in such times. The quiet words, the lengthy silences, the dark hospital room literally entombed this young woman. After one conversation, she blurted out her self-condemnation. "What I've done can never be forgiven." In my rational but private and thankfully silent agreement with her, the words came from me, "only Jesus can." "Only Jesus can" were words I was not giving as a pat answer to a terrible tragedy. They just came from somewhere. Is that the utterance of the Holy Spirit in a blank, numb and empty moment? Are we who are "word people" of a "mouth house" church, sometimes at a loss for words? And then, where do the words come from? She was not churched. To this day, her story accompanies me somewhere attached to my memory bank. I wonder about her. Pastors so often carry a part of someone's story but it is unfinished and we do not know. We fantasize about heaven being a time and place to see how parts of the human drama are resolved. We long for and hope for that day of restoration, reconciliation and resolution. And I think of the ministry of chaplains in so many of our institutional settings. They will not follow someone back out into the wide world of "normalcy;" they just serve in Christ's name where they are and cannot go further than the front door of the institution in which they serve. They are pastors, so often, of crisis. How I admire those servants of a specific time and place. Yet it is one of the reasons I wanted to serve in the parish; there would be longer years of knowing and living into many chapters of stories with parishioners. But I do so admire those "first line responders" to crisis ministry.

The young woman I remember spoke contrition about her deep sin and guilt. What then was to be spoken back to her? The church tells the truth. No one would say "don't worry, be happy." No one would say, "it'll be alright." No one would say "into every life a little rain must fall." No one would say of her dead mother, "she's in a better place." No one would say, "it must have been her time" or worse, "God took her." All these trite, worldly, counterfeit phrases were garbage in that moment. "I have done this terrible thing," is contrition. "Only Jesus can take this on," is absolution.

When the first bishop of the E.L.C.A. tells the story of his young college student son who committed suicide, he describes the depth of despair when he speaks about "hitting bottom." It's a place where we can't go any lower; it's that place beyond depression where true despair resides. "Then," he says, "I found that grace was deeper yet." So many of us comfortable Americans do a bit of trifling play with sins; they are the little, minor irritations we wish we could flip away like a mosquito. We just want a "little something," to make us feel that things will be alright and we'll be better tomorrow. "A little confession is good for the soul?" But when we deal with life and death matters, when we have nothing of ourselves to work it out, fix it or make it right; when the terror of sin has really done us to death, then there is only Jesus. From him alone there is incredible good news, "I therefore declare to you, in the mercy and grace of Christ Jesus, the entire forgiveness of all your sins, in the name of the Father and of the Son and of the Holy Spirit," "Your sin is forgiven, arise and walk!" "Go in Peace, serve the Lord . . ."

In repentance and forgiveness, we see again as in others articles of the Augsburg Confession, that there is simply a word to be proclaimed. We think words are cheap, easy and worthless. Not this word. This word of life is the powerful word of new creation just as God's first word brought forth this entire creation from atom to universe. "Just a word" so powerful that it's whole content is Jesus, crucified, dead, buried, resurrected and ascended so that this word is life's word, forgiveness's word, grace's word . . . exploding limitations, setting free from sin, death and the grave, opening new life to new times and new places. And that is what "being born from above" is all about. Thanks be to God!

After the long and arduous conversation with the young woman, I remember pushing open the hospital door on a late summer day and feeling the sun's light and warmth meet me in the exit from that place. I remember feeling the breeze against my cheek that day as though I had never experienced such a thing before. It was a walk into something new that day; it was a day full of grace in spite of all the deep, deep trouble. Contrition is the script we write. Absolution is the word God speaks in the face of it all.

It remains a great mystery to me that some would have us sidestep the whole notion of "repentance." Two American icons threw down this gauntlet towards American denominations who show no repentance about their lives, behaviors and inactions with these words: first,

H. Richard Niebuhr, saying we want "a God without wrath, who brought people without sin into a kingdom without judgment through the ministrations of a Christ without a cross." (The Kingdom of God in America, New York, Harper, 1937, p. 193).

Or, this by Billy Sunday about Christians in need of conversion (in Jordan's 95 Theses, Thesis 29): "Hog-jowled, weasel-eyed, sponge-columned, mushy-fisted, jelly-spined, pussy-footing, four flushing, Charlotte-russe Christians." Thus, the truth-telling we need to hear and more to the point, the truth-telling we need to do: confession and repentance.

Questions for Reflection

- Can you share a time when God's forgiveness has been most real for you?

- Can repentance stand alone or is there always a need to try "and make things right?'

- Do we really trivialize or dismiss the word of absolution?

- What are the times when you have declared an absolution to another person?

Article 13

"Concerning the Use of Sacraments"

> *Concerning the use of sacraments they teach that sacraments were instituted not only to be marks of profession among human beings but much more to be signs and testimonies of God's will toward us, intended to arouse and strengthen faith in those who use them. Accordingly, sacraments are to be used so that faith, which believes the promises offered and displayed through the sacraments, may increase.*

THE STORY is told of Martin Luther that there were those times of despondency and terrible doubt (he would call it the "onslaught of the devil") that the only thing he might cling to was a covenant promise given to him by God, and so, he would shout, "I am baptized!" There are those moments when reminder of our identity is needed. There are those times when we need an awakening and a confirmation of *who* we are and *whose* we are. A salesperson away from home for stretches of time or a military person on a long deployment might wander into a place of drink and entertainment and be tempted in various ways to "numb the memory," and succumb to the chants of "eat, drink and be merry." Sometimes, the wedding ring might best be felt as a "remembrance" of identity and loyalty and love. The ring of course has little to do with the entirety of the marriage but it is an outward sign that awakens the fact and confirms the identity of one in such a way as to honor the covenant as wife and husband. So too the sacraments are "signs" of grace coming to us with audible word and visible sign. The sign itself is not what is worshipped or adored. There was and is great protestant antipathy toward the Corpus Christi processions that give adoration or even a sense of worship of the elements of Holy Communion. And yet such "signs" with the Word are the very "means" of the conveyance of the gifts of forgiveness, life and salvation. The Sacraments put before us another instance of the Word going incarnational, the Word takes on flesh. The Word with the "stuff" (words, bread, wine and water) commanded by Jesus deliver his very life to a faithful recipient. To believe such powerful words and signs is the very gift of faith.

I remember two adults in a former parish, one middle aged and one elderly who came to me with similar stories: they were orphaned early in life, had no other family and yet had been raised in the church and were faithful also in their adult lives with worship attendance and involvements. With all the "faithful" responses they made, there was a lingering question and a nagging doubt they carried with them: had they once-upon-a-time been baptized? There was no certificate, no parish record; could they have assumed such was the case? And then the questions from both: "can I be baptized; I am not sure I ever was baptized." I am thankful that a seminary faculty member had once shared this scenario in class and said something about "provisional baptism;" in other words, go ahead and perform the sacrament with the words, "if you have not already been baptized, then I baptize you "in the Name of the Father and of the Son and of the Holy Spirit." What the person longs for is the assurance that the sign brings. The sign is that external pledge of God's spoken covenant. It is like the "ring in marriage," it awakens and confirms the reality and truth of the covenant promised in the Word. When in doubt, we too may cling to a shouted passion, "I am baptized!"

Questions for Reflection

- When you see a baptism in the church's worship, what memories/thoughts/reflections go through your mind?

- What is your understanding of receiving our living Lord with the bread and wine of Holy Communion?

- Do the outward signs matter in the life of faith?

- How would you define a sacrament and how has the church taught it?

"Concerning Church Order"

Concerning church order they teach that no one should teach publicly in the church or administer the sacraments unless properly called.

OUR CHURCH today is in the dilemma of re-interpreting this article but with the provision still of the original intent of "good order." Today there are expanded missional needs of the church that argue for assistance in both preaching and administration of the sacraments. The truth is that there are many vacant congregations across the church who have no full time pastor to preach or preside. There are also many congregations with large numbers of shut-ins, nursing home and homebound parishioners who would like more frequent visitation and administration of the sacrament than the one pastor can provide. Thus, the missional necessities have brought forth creative use of laity as assisting ministers in these instances. Many of our bishops have constructed training programs for "synodically authorized ministers" as allowed in the 1993 church-wide assembly adoption of the "Study on Ministry" of the E.L.C.A. These appointed lay assistants are trained, authorized and supervised to provide a limited but necessary function in a vacant, local parish for the preaching of the Word and the administration of the sacraments. The Bishop supervises such administration through her/his office and usually includes specified time frames, allowances, etc. Likewise, in many congregations, the hope for increased visitation and sacrament availability to the home-bound, has resulted in pastors appointing and training lay communion assistants who take the sacrament from the church's worship to the homes of parishioners either monthly or weekly, depending on the church's Eucharistic schedule. This too is administered from the pastoral office and is for limited and specific needs.

Also, Pastors, in our tradition, have often encouraged the laity to preach not on a regular basis but on special occasions such as Lenten worship or Youth Sundays. Since this too would reside in the oversight of the pastoral office, the sermons have been discussed and perused in order to encourage the faithful proclamation of the Gospel of Jesus Christ (it is still the pastor's responsibility for what is said from the pulpit). I have always believed that every one of God's baptized children has a sermon to preach. Most are spoken in the other six days of the week when the "pulpit" is the checkout counter or the gas pump or the boardroom or the nursing station or the sports field or the playground. The "living word" goes forth in individual witness and testimony in the lives of God's faithful people.

This article 14 is related to article 5 "on the ministry of the church." God has provided an office of Word and Sacrament ministry for the sake of getting the justifying Word of grace out to the people and to the world in worship. Thus, the Bishop or Pastor in the place bears great responsibility (and our church interprets this as a potential "shared responsibility") to see that the Word is proclaimed and the Sacraments are administered each week in the worship rhythm of the parish. And for the sake of "good order," such "oversight" is protected and projected by a regular, public call. Some person is called for such oversight and supervision.

Historically, during the time of the Reformation, the Lutheran insight phrased in the "priesthood of all believers" meant that other left wing movements could endorse many persons preaching and teaching and these things did begin to happen. Self-appointed preachers roamed the church and countryside. Many descendents of the "self appointed" would find a friendly environment in later settlements in the U.S. Hence, in reaction to any misunderstandings, the Augsburg Confession would use this article to prohibit such freelancing apart from the church. A regular call of the church was necessary for preaching of the Word and administration of the Sacraments.

Questions for Reflection

- Can anyone preach and administer the sacraments; why or why not?

- What would you say are the *daily* venues for lay preaching?

- What "assisting functions" serve parishioners in your congregation?

- In an ICU, medical personnel sometimes baptize in emergencies at the request of family. If emergency circumstances make such allowance are there other such moments?

Article 15

"Concerning Church Rites"

Concerning church rites they teach that those rites should be observed that can be observed without sin and that contribute to peace and good order in the church, for example, certain holy days, festivals, and the like. However, people are reminded not to burden consciences, as if such worship were necessary for salvation. They are also reminded that human traditions that are instituted to win God's favor, merit grace, and make satisfaction for sins are opposed to the gospel and the teaching of faith. That is why vows and traditions concerning foods and days, etc., instituted to merit grace and make satisfaction for sins, are useless and contrary to the gospel.

For the older folk among us, there is recall about our Roman Catholic friends and the pressures they lived under prior to Vatican II reforms. The "meatless" Fridays or the "fish on Fridays" for Roman Catholics was a mandatory rule; likewise, attendance at Mass and official holy days was mandated. Children were terrified at the thought of meat on Friday, a missed confession or Mass or even entry into a protestant church. Imagine my surprise when I served a parish in Grand Rapids, MI and a Roman Catholic nun called me and inquired, "what are Lutherans doing on Reformation Sunday?" I replied, "we'll be having festival worship; would you like to come?" "We cannot on Sunday morning, but would you have anything in the afternoon or evening?" "We will now," I answered.

And so it was that the congregation heard of this request and planned an ecumenical vespers worship on the festival Sunday of Reformation. At the conclusion of the worship, the nuns were filing out and an 85 year old sister, tugged at my alb sleeve and said, "two things about today: this is my first time ever in a protestant church!" And, with a twinkle in her eye, she said, "second thing, there's not much difference is there?" We bonded or at least "bridged" on that festival day. What an occasion to receive an entire convent of nuns as special guests for a worship liturgy and yet what a commentary that this was her first visit *ever* to a protestant church.

Surrounding the Roman Catholic Church at the time of the Reformation was a definitive self-protecting dictate about what was necessary for faithful adherents. Among such necessities were dietary rules, behavior rules, and attendance rules. To believe that one's eternal salvation or damnation could revolve around one's success or failure to fulfill such obligatory commands became a major theme in the "justification vs. good works" axis of debate and deliberation. A person's failures in prescribed areas could be mortal sins punishable according to church determinations. As Anglicans arrived in the new world, rules of church attendance were rigorously enforced by the English as well. A flogging, confinement to the stocks or worse, could be administered in the case of worship absence. Against this rigidity came protestant freedom.

There have been times when this pastor has wished that the "threat of enforcement" was a Protestant principle. Instead we have this "freedom" notion about the Gospel as invitation. It is noticed that Catholic churches have packed parking lots compared to Protestant "space available" circumstances. As a parent, your child will confront you with a question, "why must I go to church again when I already know the story?" It that moment, there is temptation to decree that "to miss is a mortal sin," and go ahead and strike terror into the child's consciousness! When we were asked that very question by our children, "why do I have to go to church," we answered, "because Jesus expects it." That seemed to suffice for some years at least. Of greater importance was the parental example and model of the understanding that we do this together; this is our Sunday morning routine and it is of great importance to us, to Jesus, and to the church. Still, this notion of command/demand or invitation/freedom axis has specific historical antecedents as reformation point and counterpoint. We sigh deeply today knowing that freedom too often has become reckless libertarianism. We also know that strict obedience may conform and constrict our outer behavior but cannot affect the heart and motives of persons on the interior! Still, in Article 15, the Reformers insisted that anything smacking of a way of salvation beyond the Gospel of Jesus Christ, even if proclaimed by the church, was anathema!

Questions for Reflection

- Our churches have "C & E" (Christmas and Easter) Christians. What expectations do we have for worship/sacrament attendance?

- When a person says "I can worship God (fill in the blank: on a golf course, at the mountain cabin or at the shore)," what are the discussion points and caveats of such a statement?

- Ought not our churches have high expectations for discipleship? Why or why not?

- What are the expectations of members within this congregation? How does it infringe upon the freedom of the Gospel?

"Concerning Civic Affairs"

Concerning civic affairs they teach that lawful civil ordinances are good works of God and that Christians are permitted to hold civil office, to work in law courts, to decide matters by imperial and other existing laws, to impose just punishments, to wage just war, to serve as soldiers, to make legal contracts, to hold property, to take an oath when required by magistrates, to take a wife, to be given in marriage.

THE QUESTION has been around for centuries: if you are a called, chosen person of God, therefore a citizen of God's kingdom, what are you to do when the kingdom of this world makes some demands on your life, your time, allegiance and money? Jesus undergoes an "entrapment" question when the Pharisees ask him, "is it lawful to pay taxes?" When Jesus asks for a coin and questions whose image is on it, his reply is "give to Caesar what belongs to Caesar and to God what belongs to God," (Luke 20: 22–25). Again, in the interview before Pilate, he speaks about his kingdom not being a kingdom of this world (John 18:36). So the dilemma is this: what allegiances to what kingdom? Luther saw that the world's kingdom was very much a gift of God in the sense that provision was made for law, order and peace. Just as persons in various vocations had a place from God to work and serve, so too the structures of the kingdom of this world serve to give protection from enemies and provide peaceful order in which the well being of all peoples is promoted. Luther was not a person who saw democracies, middle classes or capitalism on the scene of his 16th century stage! There was no citizen participation or vote. Benevolent rule depended on the personality of individual princes. With such caveats named, one cannot produce a Luther "make-over" into a modern citizen. We can say that he believed that God was the giver of government structure and that a citizen did indeed "owe" an allegiance to the upholding of a social order whether deferring to marriage laws, military or magisterial service. Other reformation movements would exclude such citizenship and rather condemn such participation in a social order. One such sect that landed in America and continues to practice such separatist behaviors are the "Amish." Their strict interpretation of God's kingdom call causes them to separate and isolate from surrounding society and culture. The two poles in Christendom continue to exist: those who see no contradiction between Christian faith and citizenship and those who say it's one or the other. For Lutherans, Article 16, upholds the participation of Christians in matters of the civil state.

I had a long tenure in serving a congregation near the Naval base in Norfolk, VA. Many of the folk in that congregation were officers. While there were a handful of hard core conservatives, I was most surprised at a majority of liberal (in the best sense of the word!) and expansive thinking of many of the fine officers I met. Women and men in the military had a fine grasp of their own dedications and devotions to church and state that was exemplary in so many ways. Many of the Christians stressed a devotion to "peacekeeping" and defense rather than gung-ho aggression. They spoke of "restraint" and proportional response to aggression. The church building had a flag and "remembrance of veterans" in the narthex, but not in the nave. They expected the worship area to be free from national symbols and saw the sanctuary as a different "turf" with global perspective beyond a national one. And most surprisingly, one of the officer/leaders said, "Pastor, I would not expect my church to elevate any national holiday above the Sunday worship/festival or season of the Church year." I thankfully never felt any pressure about Memorial Day, Veterans Day or the 4th of July. Many pastors and many congregations do. It is a tribute to the Norfolk congregation that a different vision was at work acknowledging that no pressure ought to be brought to bear on the life of the Christian Church in endorsing any political or nationalistic course. Rather, the hope was that the Church would remain free, critical, prophetic and challenging to our own nation/state in order to proclaim the vision of Jesus no matter what. There was even a radical commentary that we learn to pray for our enemies! Such folks represented the best in both Christian formation and military training. We may not live beyond nationalism until someday a President would venture to sign off a public address and not say, "God bless America," but rather, "May God bless all the peoples of our world." Then, perhaps, the larger vision will be underway for the truth of the Gospel!

At the same time, Lutherans need to indulge in self-reflection about two facts of public life. Some historians would posit the rise of Nazism in Germany to a kind of Lutheran passivism with regard to the state. How could Christians blindly align themselves with such maniacal destruction in the rise of the third reich? If God ordains the state and one may give allegiance to it, what are its limits? How do individuals stand up, speak out and protest when the state is absolutely wrong? The state always has the tools of information control and powerful manipulation and intimidation that need to be understood, questioned and confronted.

Also, in our present day U.S.A., Lutherans are vastly underrepresented in political offices. Why? Even as the seeds of reformation battles and nation-state revolutions were seen in 16th century Europe and many fled to the "new world," vowing never to participate in such wars again (my own ancestors were included in such an early exodus from Germany), did the Church seem then to adopt a passive stance of citizen involvement? Is there a deep seeded aversion to public policies and office holding? A wider discussion about such implications is warranted.

Questions for Reflection

- What allegiances does a citizen "owe" his/her country?

- Have you ever been a part of a large protest? If not, is there any issue that would move you to take such action?

- Why do you think Lutherans are under-represented in political offices?

- What visions of Jesus are worth the risk taking of public speech and action?

"Concerning the Return of Christ for Judgment"

They also teach that at the consummation of the world Christ will appear for judgment and will bring to life all the dead. He will give eternal life and endless joy to the righteous and elect, but he will condemn the ungodly and the devils to endless torment.

FROM CHILDHOOD on, we hear these threats in a "loving" way:

1. "Just wait till your father comes home and we'll see what he has to say about that."

2. "Let's wait and see what your report card shows us at the end of the semester."

3. "Those of you who practice a lot and show improvement, may get to: get in the game, advance in the 'chair' position in band or orchestra or get the lead part in the Spring play."

4. "I am anxious and stressed out because next week I have my annual evaluation at work."

5. "The doctor now has all the tests and will let me know what to do."

In each and every one of these cases the penultimate judgment is coming at the conclusion of days or weeks or semesters. In the meantime, the threat of the judgment is meant to shape behavior in the present! "Do what you are supposed to do, in the meantime." Practice more, work harder, change your life in some way, J-day is coming! The implicit message is, "shape up or ship out." Now everyone knows that back in the day of father/bread-winner/single parent working household ("Father knows best" television show) that when poor 'ol Pop walked in, what was he to do? Mom would tell him about something that happened two hours earlier, so was he supposed to double her anger and dish out punishment or, how could he look at this recently reformed angelic countenance of the child in front of him and do anything but love that child? Since he was not privy to all the electrically charged atmosphere that had gone on two hours earlier, was he simply to execute punishment or rather enjoy the child? My father was much more gentle and easy-going than was the whole stress and anticipation of thinking of him as a judge and executioner during those two terrible intermittent hours! So, had the threat of punishment worked to change behavior or had patient waiting diffused and therefore changed the whole atmosphere?

The church, and its teaching about the last judgment, has often affected behaviors by literally scaring the hell out of people! Martin Luther biographically tells of a church that presented such a judging, damning God and that the discovery of "grace" in Christ Jesus was transformative not just for his life but also for subsequent Christian history! The scare tactic is still rampant in fundamentalist churches today and several televangelists proclaim that natural disasters are obviously God's judgment upon the sins of certain populations. Whether or not God's judgments break into our personal histories is a question for deep theological reflection. Article 17 is not about penultimate judgment by Christ but rather about the ultimate and final one. Obviously, in this life, our behaviors, deeds and actions are very important and influential in human existence. It all has a rather dynamic quality about it. One of my favorite sayings from Luther is this:

> . . . this life therefore is *not* righteousness but growth in righteousness;
>
> *not* health but healing;
>
> *not* being but becoming;
>
> *not* rest but exercise;
>
> We are *not* yet what we shall be but we are growing toward it,
>
> the process is *not* yet finished but it is going on,
>
> this is *not* the end but it is the road.
>
> All does *not* yet gleam in glory but all is being purified.[1]

In a post-communion prayer from the Lutheran Book of worship, we pray these words: "Almighty God, you gave your Son both as a sacrifice for sin and model of the godly life. Enable us to receive him always with thanksgiving, and to *conform* our lives to his; through the same Jesus Christ our Lord. Amen." There is much work to do on this side of judgment day to conform not only our lives but our world to the life of Jesus. This becomes a truly prophetic vision with social and political implications. The word from Article 17 is both threat and promise. There will be, at the end, a "J-day" when evil, devils and the ungodly are vanquished. There's the threat. But also there is a coming "J-day" meaning "Jesus' day" who comes with healing and grace and the ultimate fullness and completion of God's love bestowed in "eternal life and joy." Such is the abiding promise toward which all Christians and the whole creation groan in the birth pangs of new creation!

(As an aside, Dr. Nelson Strobert, Gettysburg Seminary Professor of Christian Education, shared a copy of an early Sunday School paper published by the "Orphans' Home, Germantown, PA, called "The Busy Bee." It is a collection of inspirational sto-

---

1. "Luther, *Works, Vol. 32*, 24.

ries for young people to read. The edition from Nov. 10, 1866, included the following: "History, from the German of Caspari: 'The Most Important Question:'

A carefree and thoughtless youth once came in great haste to his father, a pious old man and said, "Father, rejoice with me; I have, at last, obtained the consent of my uncle to enter college, after which I wish to be a lawyer. Now my fortune is made." "Excellent my son," replied the father; "then you can begin at once to apply yourself diligently to your studies; but—what then?" "In three years I shall pass an examination—be crowned with honor,—leave college and enter upon my profession." "What then?" "I shall not be wanting in industry or conscientiousness; people will hear of me far and near; and all, both rich and poor, will gladly repose confidence in me." "What then?" "Then I shall begin to save in order to become a rich man; I shall marry an estimable wife, and regulate my household with care." "What then?" "I will educate my children in such a manner that they too may be useful in the world—each one according to the talents he possesses. Of course, they will prosper if they move in their father's footsteps." "Well, what then?" "Then I shall retire from business to enjoy the prosperity and love of my children, and thus prepare myself for a happy old age." "And then?" "Then?—well, people cannot live here forever, and if they could, it would not be desirable—then, indeed!—well, then I suppose I must die." "And then!" solemnly repeated the father, seizing both his hands and earnestly looking into his face; "my son!—and then?" At those words, the thoughtless youth grew pale, and began to tremble, while the hot tears coursed rapidly down his cheeks. "Thank you, dear father," he said at last; "I forgot the most important of all—that 'it is appointed for man once to die, and then the judgment.' But from today, I promise to show no more indifference for the 'chief concern of life.'"

Can anyone among us imagine this 1866 story being told today? The very sense of the return of Christ for judgment is a bygone relic or is it?

Questions for Reflection

- Does anyone today consider a vision of a final judgment?

- Does impending judgment influence present behaviors and actions?

- A bumper sticker slogan has said, "Jesus is coming soon . . . look busy." In light of Article 17, what should our busy-ness be about?

- How do you put into words and images a vision of "eternal life and endless joy" and all we mean by the term "heaven?"

ARTICLE 18

"Concerning Free Will"

Concerning free will they teach that the human will has some freedom for producing civil righteousness and for choosing things subject to reason. However, it does not have the power to produce the righteousness of God or spiritual righteousness without the Holy Spirit, because "those who are natural do not receive the gifts of God's Holy Spirit" (I Cor. 2: 14). But this righteousness is worked in the heart when the Holy Spirit is received through the Word. In Book III of Hypognosticon Augustine says this in just so many words: "We confess that all human beings have a free will that possesses the judgment of reason. It does not enable them, without God, to begin—much less complete—anything that pertains to God, but only to perform the good or evil deeds of this life. By 'good deeds' I mean those that arise from the good in nature, that is, the will to labor in the field, to eat and drink, to have a friend, to wear clothes, to build a house, to marry, to raise cattle, to learn various useful skills, or to do whatever good pertains to this life. None of these exists without divine direction; indeed, from him and through him they have come into being and exist. However, by 'evil deeds' I mean the will to worship an idol, to commit murder, etc."

MODERN PEOPLE (at least in democratic countries) celebrate freedom and independence. Such post-Enlightenment philosophies crashed onto the world scene and continue to bubble and stir in the hearts and minds of people around the globe. The freedom to think, act and choose are precious legacies born of revolutionary actions and philosophical constructs that have not always been a "given." In the span of human history, it is remarkable to think that this article in the Augsburg Confession coming almost two and half centuries before the American revolution, could speak of humanity's "free will" and trace such words back to St. Augustine. There is a notion about what each person can "choose" to think and do. Article 18 agrees with this when considering our actions in matters of our civil or social life. We have the "judgment of reason;" we have some freedom for producing "civil righteousness" according to such reasonable thinking and decisions. This assurance is a refreshing stance in light of so many multi-cultural/multi-religious populations that must forge some agreements on how to govern and how to live. The search for the "reasonable" informed by our freedom is a treasured possession of societal functioning. Much of the Jeffersonian experiment was proposing for all time that "certain truths are self-evident," and gave a vision and trajectory to protect and nurture human freedom and its relationship to government. It is refreshing too in a time and place where some "Christians" want to stamp the U.S. as a Judeo-Christian nation. Luther would insist that it would not be necessary for social well being that the emperor be Christian but that the ruler should be able to reason. His words: "Christians are not needed for secular authority. Thus it is not necessary for the emperor to be a saint. It is not necessary for him to be a Christian to rule. It is sufficient for the emperor to possess reason."[1] This is a radical idea in an age that insists on a faith litmus test of its candidates for national office! Rather, good "reason" is the most significant quality in a leader.

1. Luther, "Sermon, 1528," 417–18.

While insisting that a person's deeds according to reason, may be "good" or "evil," article 18 is mostly insistent about a theological point: nothing in the life of faith is according to our free "will" to choose but rather, all things in the life of faith come, not of our choice or will, but solely by the Holy Spirit. Any and all things of God come where the Holy Spirit wills and wishes such birth and growth. Since the overwhelming majority of Christendom finds itself in the matrix of Roman, Orthodox, Lutheran, Anglican and Calvinist churches, the question of "when did you find Jesus?" or, "when were you saved?" is an alien and unknown idea to these churches. The rather unique phenomena in the U.S. from the "great awakening" to the penchant for "revivals" and "crusades" spins this theological perspective on its ear! Rather, what is stressed in article 18 is the complete inability of people to choose or will faith. Faith is a gift given by the Holy Spirit; we are chosen (i.e., we don't do the choosing), we are birthed, we are graced by the Holy Spirit who "calls, gathers, enlightens and sanctifies" those whom the Spirit wills. We cannot "birth" ourselves or "gift" ourselves; these must be done to us. Likewise, in the matter of faith, this too is pure gift and not an act of our own doing, choosing, or believing. What God then chooses to do to us, at us and for us, overwhelms the recipient with such love and grace that we know this to be "not of our own doing," but only by the grace, love and mercy of God. There is neither initiation nor cooperation on our part for such faith. One can only receive, thankfully acknowledge, and then praise, glorify and serve God in response to such a gift. One of the great chasms in the church is around this very question: in faith, is the chief actor God or us? Can this be self-initiated and therefore a matter of free will and choice or is everything God initiated? Response to this question guides much in how a person reflects and thinks about faith. Article 18 is clear about good "reason" in service to most everything in life *except* faith, and this can only be the work of the Holy Spirit!

Questions for Reflection

- How do you respond to another's question: "when were you saved?"

- Is there a source of "good deeds/evil deeds" as you understand it?

- Must this country always consider the faith of its candidates to be a test for public office?

- What shall we say about moments in church history when revivals and/or reformations have truly renewed the church? Is this too not a work of the Holy Spirit?

"Concerning the Cause of Sin"

> *Concerning the cause of sin they teach that although
> God creates and preserves nature, nevertheless the
> cause of sin is the will of those who are evil, that is,
> of the devil and the ungodly. Since it was not assisted
> by God, their will turned away from God, as Christ
> says in John 8: 44, "when (the devil) lies, he speaks
> according to his own nature."*

INSURANCE COMPANIES contain clauses in policies that refer to "acts of God." Poor God gets the blame for all that goes wrong in nature. Both the stupidity and the complicity of human beings are so often left out of the conversation. We have good friends who own ocean beachfront property. It is a cottage with a wonderful view and the sounds of crashing waves become a bedtime lullaby for guests. Every summer, in addition to the enjoyment of hosting many guests, the season also comes to be a time of high stress due to hurricane season. Twice in the last thirty years, the cottage has been totally or partially destroyed. Perched on fragile sand dunes, the insurance company defines an "act of God" in such a way that payments are given (after all, isn't that what insurance is for?) and the couple who own that lot re-build again and anxiously watch for the next season of ocean storms! If God has certain cycles of nature that even involve rain and winds and sun and snow, who interferes? If God re-arranges a shore line and sends rivers in new directions, who interferes with nature's meanderings? We do!

God has gifted the earth with clean air and water and we have dumped chemicals into streams and belched smoke into the air so that the poisons affect life and delicate balances which we ignore. Our stewardship is squandered and we are most to be pitied! Such sin tears apart what God has given and arranged in its intricate balances and the culprit is each and every one of us. And the list goes on . . .

- we push the pedal to the metal and crash the car;
- we take up drugs/alcohol and chemicals and wreck the body;
- we make and use guns and armaments to kill and destroy;
- we hurl thoughtless, angry words to hurt and wound others;
- we violate the boundaries of God and choose to step into adultery, language and behaviors, theft, greed and covetousness when God has clearly said, "don't go there."

And then the public lament is heard again in some theologically grounded plea, "why did God let this happen?" Most of the evil that befalls us comes in two categories: some is obviously about "cause and effect," and we can see and know *why* this bad thing happened. "He was intoxicated and his speeding with the car spun it out of control." Still, the grief and the pain of the surviving family are great. Other evil things are totally mysterious and we shall never know. The pre-school child has a deadly cancer and dies. There is no known "cause and effect," only a mystery and we shall not know why. Still, the grief and the pain of the surviving family are great.

Article 19 wants us to remember that while our God is the God of life, there is an opponent of God let loose in our world (of unknown origin or simply the unity of all human evil?), this power of sin, death and evil has been called "devil." And while mythic symbols abound and we laugh at the idea of a figure with horns and a pitch fork, the reality of the "evil one" does indeed capture a reality almost beyond our description and most certainly beyond our knowing. Much of the evil we encounter does center in the decisions and choices of our free will gone bad. But perceptive people know too, that there is a permeation of evil that is beyond human agency and whatever "that" is, we have labeled, defined and described it as the "devil," or the one who prowls around like a lion seeking to devour. Such origins are speculative and therefore not addressed in this article; only the empirical fact of evil derived of human agency is addressed and that is *not* of God but of persons.

Questions for Reflection

- What "devil" caricatures do we carry with us?

- We are an "answer/solution" seeking people. Do we really allow for not having an answer to tragedy? Would it not be better to sometimes keep our mouths shut rather than offer trite phrases to a grieving person (such as "it must have been their time," or, "God took him for a reason?")

- How do you speak of evil to a child? How do we hope to protect them from harm?

- Does your personal confession speak of your complicity in evil and death?

Article 20

"Concerning Faith and Good Works"

Our people are falsely accused of prohibiting good works. For their writings on the Decalogue and others on similar subjects bear witness that they have given useful instruction concerning all kinds and walks of life: what manner of life and which activities in every calling please God. In former times preachers taught too little about such things. Instead, they urged childish and needless works, such as particular holy days and fasts, brotherhoods, pilgrimages, the cult of saints, rosaries, monasticism and the like. Since our adversaries have been reminded about these things, they are now unlearning them and do not preach about such useless works as much as in former times. They are also beginning to mention faith, about which there once was an astonishing silence. They teach that we are not justified by works alone, but they combine faith and works, saying that we are justified by both. This teaching is more tolerable than the previous one and can offer more consolation than their old teaching.

Therefore, because the teaching concerning faith, which ought to be the principal one in the church, has languished so long in obscurity—everyone must grant that here has been a profound silence concerning the righteousness of faith in preaching while only the teaching of works has been promoted in the church—our people have instructed the churches about faith in the following way:

To begin with, they remind the churches that our works cannot reconcile God or merit grace and forgiveness of sins, but we obtain this only by faith when we believe that we are received into grace on account of Christ, who alone has been appointed mediator and atoning sacrifice through whom the Father is reconciled. Therefore, all who trust that they merit grace by works despise the merit and grace of Christ and seek a way to God without Christ through human powers, since Christ has said about himself (John 14:6a), "I am the way, and the truth and the life."

This teaching concerning faith is treated by Paul everywhere. Ephesians 2: 8–9: "For by grace you have been saved through faith, and this is . . . not the result of works . . ."

So that no one may quibble that we have contrived a new interpretation of Paul, this entire approach is supported by the testimonies of the Fathers. In many writings Augustine defends grace and the righteousness of faith against the merit of works. Ambrose teaches similar things in "Concerning the Calling of the Gentiles" and elsewhere. For in "Concerning the Calling of the Gentiles" he says: "Redemption by the blood of Christ would become worthless and the preference for human works would not give way to the mercy of God if justification, which takes place by grace, were due to antecedent merits. For then it would be the worker's wage rather than the donor's gift."

Moreover, although this teaching is despised by those without experience, nevertheless devout and anxious consciences find by experience that it offers the greatest consolation. For consciences cannot be calmed by any work, but only by faith when they are certain that they have a God who has been reconciled on account of Christ. As Paul teaches in Romans 5:1: "Therefore, since we are justified by faith, we have peace with God." This whole teaching must be referred to that struggle of the terrified conscience, and it cannot be understood apart from that struggle. That is why those who are wicked and without experience judge it badly. For they imagine that Christian righteousness is nothing but civil and philosophical righteousness.

In former times, consciences were vexed by the doctrine of works; they did not hear consolation from the gospel. Conscience drove some into the desert, into monasteries, where they hoped to merit grace through the monastic life. Some contrived other works to merit grace and make satisfaction for sins. Consequently, it was essential to pass on and restore this teaching about faith in Christ so that anxious consciences should not be deprived of consolation but know that grace and forgiveness of sins are apprehended by faith in Christ.

People are also reminded that the term "faith" here does not signify only historical knowledge—the kind of faith that the ungodly and the devil have—but that it signifies faith believes not only the history but also the effect of the history, namely, this article of the forgiveness of sins, that is, that we have grace, righteousness, and forgiveness of sins through Christ.

Now all who know that they are reconciled to the Father through Christ truly know God, know that God cares for them, and call upon him. In short, they are not without God, as are the heathen. For the devils and the ungodly cannot believe this article of the forgiveness of sins. Hence they hate God as an enemy, do not call upon him, and expect nothing good from him. Augustine also reminds his readers in this way about the word "faith" and teaches that in the Scriptures the word "faith" is to be understood *not as knowledge, such as the ungodly have, but as trust that consoles and encourages terrified minds.*

Beyond this, our people teach that it is necessary to do good works, not that we should count on meriting grace through them but because it is the will of God. It is only by faith that forgiveness of sins and grace are apprehended. Moreover, because the Holy Spirit is received through faith, consequently hearts are renewed and endowed with new affections so as to be able to do good works. For Ambrose says, "Faith is the mother of the good will and the righteous action." For without the Holy Spirit human powers are full of ungodly affections and are too weak to do good works before God. Besides, they are under the power of the devil, who impels human beings to various sins, ungodly opinions, and manifest crimes. This also may be seen in the philosophers, who, though they have tried to live honestly, were still not able to do so but were defiled by many obvious crimes. Such is the weakness of human beings when they govern themselves by human powers alone without faith or the Holy Spirit.

Hence it is readily apparent that no one should accuse this teaching of prohibiting good works. On the contrary, it is rather to be commended for showing how we can do good works. For without faith human nature cannot possibly do the works of the First or Second Commandments. Without faith it does not call upon God, expect anything from God, or bear the cross, but seeks and trusts in human help. Consequently, all kinds of urges and human designs rule in the heart when faith and trust in God are lacking. That is why Christ said (John 15:5): "Apart from me you can do nothing." And the church sings: Without your will divine/naught is in humankind/all innocence is gone.

THE SHEER length of this article shows that it was one of the main issues in the context of the Reformation. The relationship of faith and good works set theological parameters around a central controversy. Lutherans saw the issue of "doing good works," as a frequent prescription for penance handed out by a priest/confessor; this implied that a sin's penalty was satisfied when one did a good work to cancel out a sin. Lutherans saw this as contributing to the abuse or distortion of God's free grace and forgiveness given completely in Jesus Christ through his death on the cross. Meanwhile, Roman Catholics accused the Protestants of denying the benefit of any good work and accused reformers of an emphasis on faith without consequent good deeds; hence, both misunderstanding and impasse were the result.

Some of what is offered in Article 20 may seem like very familiar echoes of previous articles (see 4 and 6). But the expansion of the words in this article bring at least three main points to the fore: first, clinging to faith does not mean elimination of good works as some critics charged towards the Lutherans; second, one should consider the matter of the terrified conscience; and, third, faith is not knowledge or history but rather trust that encourages and consoles.

Concerning the "first" expansion of commentary, it seems that moderns would have a problem identifying with a peculiar Reformation context. But certain phrases of the reform movement were prevalent in Germany (even in Latin!). The phrases were: sola fidei and sola gratia: faith alone, grace alone. When these phrases trickled into Roman ears, they believed that any good works were therefore excluded from one's faith life. This article seeks to call that a misrepresentation of the Lutheran position and give correction. The article delineates again that only faith is the operative truth in regard to God and that good works have nothing to do with one's standing before God. On the other hand, following the "great commandment," one's love of God also includes one's love of neighbor. And to this end, what we do for our neighbor's good is worthy, commendable and very important. When God justifies us and our relationship with God is pure gift, we are therefore free from "religious, holy" pursuits and even more free to expend our energies in loving service to our neighbor in need. This distinction was and is, most important for Lutherans to understand again that good works do not merit or earn God's favor. Shall Lutherans and all faithful Christians do good works? Yes, by all means!

The second part of this commentary has to do with a phrase that also may be difficult for moderns to understand: how does one address the "terrified conscience?" Some decades ago, psychologist/writer Karl Menninger asked in a provocative book title, "whatever became of sin?" As a pastor of thirty years, I must say that I would use the term "terrified conscience" to describe less than a handful of personal confessional/counseling situations. And I do wonder why? Sins are so covered over today. We have so reacted against guilt, shame and personal responsibility that we don't seem to recognize our own involvement or complicity in sin's matrix. We think that we have promoted psychological health by emphasizing "self esteem" (be yourself), "self actualization" (I'm ok; you're ok) and "self discovery" (you gotta do what feels right) so that there is no terrified conscience and many would add, "nor should there be." In addition to all of these "self" interests, there is the whole matter of cover-up. This however, is simply the story in the Garden of Eden playing out once again. Adam: "Eve gave me the apple." Eve: "the serpent suggested it to me," etc. Layers of rationalization exist today and it is no wonder good psychotherapists are needed. The layers need to be explored in depth. When an entire culture drives home the thought that all of us are basically good people, we can all drift with the flow of goodness even when we make a bad call now and then. When sin is reduced to a "bad call," or a "regrettable decision" or, "I got myself into a bad situation," there is no terrified conscience. Religious communities may never return to the days when "confession is good for the soul," but if we tell the truth, it is this: only when one grasps the reality and depth of sin, can the gracious and good word of forgiveness in Christ Jesus take hold and give new life. Only then is one "born from above" like a newborn infant.

While I do remember a handful of "terrified consciences" before me at certain times in parish ministry, I remember also an attendant problem with these folks: they would often ask, after absolution was pronounced, "but can I really be forgiven?" Even immediately after God's gracious Word is proclaimed, doubt creeps in and tries to destroy what God has pronounced and we think, "God can't forgive what I've done." Liturgically, our public confession and forgiveness must be spoken often. It at least gives a mass rehearsal of this dynamic of confession and forgiveness. But our churches need to recover the usage of individual confession and forgiveness as a linkage between sin and new life. This is the very heart of the Gospel and one should press for its inclusion in parish practice.

Finally, the third point in this article presses us to discover that "faith" is not knowledge or historical knowledge; it is not a body of information about God, but is "trust" that "consoles and encourages . . ." One of the really great Reformation insights is that faith is not a repository of information, not a library of learning or a museum of history but rather a relationship with a person. To trust God, Father, Son and Holy Spirit, is to enter into a relationship. This is a dynamic relationship in which we can argue, affirm, wrestle, debate, question, protest, hate, love, detest and adore God. Like the depth of our best human friendships, such a faith relationship is asked to "endure all things, believe all things, hope all things." And the good news is that in the midst of all this "stretching to the breaking point," our baptismal promise proclaims that this relationship is forever! For me to be in God's care and God's keeping where "neither tribulation, distress, persecution, famine, nakedness, peril, the sword, or life or death or angels or principalities or things present or things to come or powers or height or depth or anything in all creation (Romans 8: 32–39) can separate us" . . . well that is the forever special relationship promised by God!

Questions for Reflection

- Does justification set us free to serve our neighbor? Is there any lingering sense that good works are forbidden or un-necessary?

- Have you experienced yourself or have you known moments of "terrified conscience" over things done and regretted or do you agree that this is "layered over" in ways we avoid personal accountability?

- Besides a "trusting relationship," are there other words or images you would use to describe faith?

- Have you ever considered your relationship to Jesus to include some of the negatives of true friendship like "anger, argument and protest?" Or, are we just taught that "nice" is expected?

Article 21

"Concerning the Cult of the Saints"

Concerning the cult of the saints they teach that saints may be remembered in order that we imitate their faith and good works, according to our calling. Thus, the emperor can imitate the example of David in waging war to drive the Turks from our native land. For both of them are kings. However, the Scripture does not teach calling on the saints or pleading for help from them. For it sets before us Christ alone as mediator, atoning sacrifice, high priest, and intercessor. He is to be called upon, and he has promised that our prayers will be heard. Furthermore, he strongly approves this worship most of all, namely, that he be called upon in all afflictions. (I John 2:1): "But if anyone does sin, we have an advocate with the Father . . ."

PEOPLE WHO are newcomers to the Lutheran Church immediately notice that so many of our churches are named for "saints." Therefore, there will be some confusion about what saints names and stories we use in the Lutheran Church. Basically, the names of "Lutheran saints," will be the names of those contained within the Scriptures; some allowance is also provided for early church patristic fathers. However, the Roman church's process for adding thousands of saints through a church system for nominating and naming has not gone forward among Lutherans. Also, this article was put forward in order to renounce what was considered a non-Scriptural understanding of saints, namely that they each had a storehouse of "merits" that one can use for one's own needs when a special saint is invoked! Thus, prayers to a saint or merits of a saint were protested as un-scriptural according to Lutherans.

In the apology to the Augsburg Confession, three benefits about saints are advanced: first, look to saints with *thanksgiving* to God for the merciful gift God has given in raising up saints to live among us. Second, look at saints in the sense of *strengthening our faith* by their life story and good example and, finally, there are good and saintly lives that are *worthy of imitation*. For these reasons, we hold special place with respect, reverence and gratitude for such lives. But we do not pray to them; we pray only to God through Christ in the Spirit; and so, the merits of "saints" have nothing to do with our salvation, only the merit of Christ alone who intercedes and saves. These were the chief points of this article.

Practically in our churches, one of the great festivals of the Church year is "All Saints" Sunday, the first Sunday in November. Early in my ministry, I had two banners made in the church, one for "birth in the Lord" through Holy Baptism and "death in the Lord," through funerals. Names were added from one All Saints Sunday to the next and these banners were used at each special worship service and then carried in procession on All Saints Sunday. Lutherans understand "saints" to be all the baptized. We are a "communion of saints" as the phrase in the creed notes. This festival worship was particularly poignant to all those who had experienced baptisms and deaths in the year past. Their names were read and punctuated with a handbell sound. This worship gave a whole congregation a "dry eyed" Sunday to reflect on the whole sweep of God's good grace in the lives of special people given to us to "know and love in our pilgrimage on earth." Names were spoken in the prayers of the Church. Often candles might be lit by family members and placed in the church in remembrance. It is a Sunday to consider special liturgical moments to consider how best to remember and give thanks.

Lutherans and other Protestants have understood that we can call a fellow baptized sister or brother "saint." It is God's designation of them as a holy one, set apart and commissioned for service in the promise of Holy Baptism. Thus, the church does not need to continue a processing for ones more holy than others. Theologian Elton Trueblood once referred to saints as the "balcony people," the ones above us and beyond us who yet cheer us on in the adventure of steadfast faith. In much of the architecture of medieval (and later) European chapels, churches and cathedrals, church builders have used the high arches and stained glass to portray the heavenward place of apostles, saints and martyrs, angels, archangels, cherubim and seraphim who watch over us and lend their encouragement to us in the church on earth. It suggests again through such art and its placement that we are the heirs with all the company of heaven who join with us in the praise and thanksgiving in all our prayers and devotion to God: Father, Son and Holy Spirit.

The festival of All Saints can be a very special time of thanksgiving for remembrance of the special people who have modeled and gifted us in our own faith lives.

Questions for Reflection

- What has the term "saint" meant to you?

- Who are the saints you most remember as faithful examples?

- When the Creeds speak of the "communion of saints," how have you thought of that phrase?

- Are there special liturgical means you might suggest in your congregation to give special attention to this festival worship?

Specific Abuses Addressed

THE MAIN body of the Augsburg Confession now concludes with Article 21 and the conclusion states that the articles present a summary of the teachings of the church and that nothing named in these articles represents a departure from either the Scriptures or the catholic faith. The Augsburg Confession then concludes with a series of "abuses" present in the Roman Church to the extent that these issues need to be raised and corrected. Here we shall not go into detail concerning the articles charged with churchly abuse but will offer a brief summary of the remaining seven articles.

ARTICLE 22

"Concerning Both Kinds"

A PRACTICE had developed in the Roman church which distributed only the bread to communicants and withheld the wine. The reformers could find no basis for this in either Scripture or in the patristic writings of the early church. Thus, the reform movement brought back the gifts of both bread and wine and saw the very words of Jesus as the mandate for such restoration of practice.

ARTICLE 23

"Concerning the Marriage of Priests"

THERE IS a citation in this article that Pope Pius II commented that there were reasons why priests do not marry but weightier reasons as to why marriage ought to again be permitted! The article continues with citations about why marriage is preferred (references to I Cor. 7:2, 9; Matt. 19:11 and Gen. 1:28). There is citation of the writer of the pastoral epistle, I Timothy 3:2 noting that a married man should be chosen to be bishop. Because celibacy is understood as a "gift," it is noted that not everyone has been given such a gift; therefore it is possible for priests to marry. Finally, the main point again is from Scripture that God has instituted marriage as "remedy against human infirmity."

Article 24

"Concerning the Mass"

THIS ARTICLE refutes the charge that reformation churches had abolished the Mass. Indeed, the churches state that the Mass is held in great reverence and regard. The abuse of the Mass is that the liturgy is often profaned and given over to monetary profit-making. Another abuse is that the Mass is considered a "work" and offering made by priests. Another abuse is that the Mass had become offered by and for individuals rather that a sacrament of the whole church. The Mass is to "console the anxious conscience." It is offered each week and on other days as there are those who desire it. The abuse factor points to the "privatization" of masses rather than the common worship experience of the congregation.

ARTICLE 25

"Concerning Confession"

CONFESSION IS not abolished by the reformers as some have charged! Confession and Absolution normally precede the reception of Holy Communion. Confession is not a matter of enumerating a listing of sins and therefore having each sin addressed; but rather confession is penitent acknowledgement of our sinful human condition. To this and to the admission of many sins, faith grasps on to the strong Word of God who promises forgiveness through Jesus Christ. Confession is retained in the churches of the reformation because of the "great benefit of absolution" and the power of God's word to free a terrified conscience.

Article 26

"Concerning the Distinction of Foods"

THIS ARTICLE points out that many customs and traditions had become "laws" by which one might merit grace and righteousness in the observance of fasts, holy days, rites and vestments. (Many of us may have grown up in Roman Catholic communities where "fish on Fridays" and obligatory holy days were necessary for faithful communicants.) Reformers wanted to clarify three things here: first, that no actions or rules or obligations should hide the clarity of the Gospel: that we can *do* nothing to merit forgiveness and righteous, rather this is the free gift of God in Christ Jesus. Second, that practices add to one's discipline in faithful living yet disciplines are not grace! Yet disciplines had fast become the penchant of the people to believe in the traditions for their own sake rather than as a practice of discipline for the spiritual journey. Third, the fact that such obligations could never be satisfactorily practiced meant that consciences were further burdened by impossible demands. The "cross bearing" of Christians is not to merit anything before God but rather as a discipline to "keep the body under control."

The article ends with the mention that many traditions are kept by the reformers including the daily lectionary readings, festival/commemorations, and yet there is freedom in human rites and traditions and they ought not burden the conscience.

ARTICLE 27

"Concerning Monastic Vows"

M ONKS AND Nuns had once entered into communal life as a voluntary association. Later, the vows of monastic life were made before children were of legal age and this was an abuse. Many had come to think that the life "under vow" was more holy than the life of the laity and therefore pleasing to God in a special way. This "separatist community" became set apart as a God-pleasing group and therefore this "good work" of such a life was commendable to God and meritorious of forgiveness and righteousness. "No," said the reformers. These communities had once been the places of study and prayer and useful things such as pastors and Bishops came from these communities. But soon the sense of serving God in a perfect way had distorted "vocation." Once again, marriage as instituted by God, is considered "less pure" than celibacy; "vocational vow" is pleasing to God and therefore meritorious of grace. Finally, it was well known that many fled to monastic life to avoid other vows (around marriage and state obligations), also debts or contracts. Such "fleeing from the world" was an escape hatch into an offering of one's life in order to please God. For all these reasons, the indictment of monastic life was questioned by the reformers. Response to God's grace was to be seen not in fleeing the world but rather in serving it in all holiness and righteousness.

Article 28

"Concerning the Church's Power"

Perhaps no article of the Augsburg Confession can have a more contemporary ring to it than this one in our modern age where there is continuing speculation about church and state issues. Listen to a portion of this article: ". . . the powers of church and civil government must not be mixed. The power of the church possesses its own command to preach the gospel and administer the sacraments. It should not usurp the other's duty, transfer earthly kingdoms, abrogate the laws of magistrates, abolish lawful obedience, interfere with judgments concerning any civil ordinances or contracts, prescribe to magistrates laws concerning the form of government that should be established. . . . in this way, our people distinguish the duties of the two powers, and they command that both be held in honor and acknowledged as a gift and blessing of God." . . . "so when asking about the jurisdiction of bishops, one must distinguish political rule from the church's jurisdiction. Consequently, according to the gospel, or, as they say, by divine right, this jurisdiction belongs to the bishops as bishops (that is, to those to whom the ministry of Word and sacraments has been committed): to forgive sins, to reject teaching that opposes the gospel, and to exclude from the communion of the church the ungodly whose ungodliness is known—doing all this not with human power but by the Word. In this regard, churches are bound by divine right to be obedient to the bishops . . ." "However, when they teach or establish anything contrary to the gospel, churches have a command from God that prohibits obedience."

In this article, argument is advanced citing the division between the power of the gospel and the power of human rule and law. Moreover, even within church, the distinction of obedience or disobedience is premised on the clarity of the gospel or the burdening of the conscience by human additions such as observances or institution of rites, ceremonies, food, holy days, ranks and orders of ministers, etc.

One gets the point, after a reading of the Augsburg Confession, that the passion and persistence and integral core of the confession is all about "gospel clarity." Christ is central to all matters of faith. Our justification and relationship to God is a free gift of grace in Christ Jesus . . . period! Let all other things about faith and church stand or fall before this foundational faith principle.

Theologian George Forell wrote in 1968 an interesting commentary on this section and said, "in light of the Augsburg Confession the clergy have responsibility to participate in political life like any other citizen. If therefore, a pastor feels conscience-bound to march in a parade, one had better obey his conscience and go. . . . This however does not mean that clergy have the right to bind the consciences of other people, even the members of their congregation on these issues. On the other hand, if members of a congregation claim that their pastor has no right to express their political convictions simply because he/she is a pastor, they are equally wrong." ("The Augsburg Confession: A Contemporary Commentary, Augsburg Publishing House, Minneapolis, 1968, p. 105–6). In a day when clergy seem to often "cross the line" to bind their church and/or followers to certain political issues, this seems especially relevant. One may seek to reflect on this dilemma of both an individual's personal conscience and a sphere of influence over a great number of people and the inferred question about a church "position" on social or political issues.

Questions for Reflection

- How does a church address a social or political issue?

- Is there such a thing as a "Christian" position or do Christians take positions and may they faithfully do so on opposite sides of an issue?

- The Roman church at times seems to threaten political leaders if their views are contrary to church teachings. What are your reflections about this matter?

- Are there instances of ministerial abuse of power today and what are the resolutions of such abuse?

Conclusion

Do ancient documents have contemporary relevance?

The Bible? Yes.

The Magna Carta? Yes.

The U.S. Constitution? Yes

The Augsburg Confession?

The latter awaits the response of the reader. For Lutherans and others influenced by the great Reformation of the Church, the ancient documents are part of the very DNA of Lutheran identity and personality. But the documents must be taken and read and thus inform the church and the parishioner who would wish to know. These conclusions may be asserted:

- the documents have their own unique context and history. Students of history will read and study the times and personalities of one of the great epochs of Christendom's story.

- the documents were pivotal in a re-forming of church. Their writers (laypersons) and signatories (laypersons) wanted first, to assert that the confession was a clear expression of the Christian faith in its historical and orthodox understanding. 21 articles were about the central tenets of Christian faith and 7 articles hoped to correct abuses in the church catholic.

- the documents were central to the matter of "correction, change and reform" of the church. "Correction" is used in the sense of aligning the church with both Scripture and tradition. "Change" was not a pejorative term but was embraced as necessary and integral to the institutional life and time of the church at this particular juncture in history. "Reform" signals that the church would never be a static institution but a living Body of Christ, dynamic, energetic, visionary in Spirit-propelled mission to all the world! Out of these documents, the church was infused with energy and vibrant passion for the Church and its teaching and mission.

• Jesus Christ is clearly at the center of the faith and all that is said or done is to his glory and honor alone. Our standing before God is purely by way of grace given by Christ to his followers. This understanding of justification is the central criteria by which all else "stands or falls" in Christian faith. All other accretions, additions or layers in the church, whether of worship and liturgy, law and custom, saints and good works or forms and structures are forever to be tested and judged according to Christ and the grace he imparts.

• The Word of God (Christ) alone is where we must cling. The Word of God is the power center for God's people. The Word (Logos) enfleshed in Jesus (embodiment) continues to come to us in the written Word (Scripture), and in the visible Word (Sacraments). The work/deed of Jesus on the cross, imparts forgiveness and new life. This is the free gift of God in Christ Jesus and is offered through the proclamation and declaration of a "word seed" planted within the lives of the faithful. Within history, there came (and comes) a time when confusion swirls around this declaration of pure, free grace. Once, the church thought it might sell indulgences to assure forgiveness. This commercial enterprise ignited the Reformation! Dr. John Donahue (Roman Catholic scholar) speaking to a forum at Ascension Lutheran Church, Towson, MD., told of his study time in Rome when he was taking some friends around St. Peter's church. After the splendorous tour with art and sculpture and magnificence, his friends stood in the plaza in awe and asked him, "how much did this cost?" He replied, "northern Europe." Today, there are those who might yet find the free gift of grace confusing as they point to the necessity to act, behave, choose and decide in a certain way in order to merit God's forgiveness. The Reformation corrective: "having received God's grace, one will wish to so love God as to want to act/behave/choose and decide according to what is right and just. Big difference!

Finally, any response that can also energize, invigorate and "lift high the cross" of Jesus Christ, will continue to be the Spirit's gift to re-form, re-new and re-create the one, holy, catholic and apostolic church. May the documents and movements of bygone centuries find new life and meaning in all that we say and do. May followers of Jesus take and read a document rooted in history but whose implications travel into our time, and so reflect and renew their commitments to follow the One who is the Way, the Truth and the Life. Thus, shall Christians be true to the One who bids us to take up our cross and follow him.

Remember the mention of the soap and spin cycle in the "Over-view" section of this book? Christian faith and Gospel have their own version of a spin cycle: a thrown upside down, turned inside out cycle of spinning, tumbling and churning! Such were the times of "Reformation." Such are the times of re-formation. When the ordinary encounters the miraculous, when the divine encounters the human, when the heavens encounter the earth, everything matters and everything changes. The fizz of grace under pressure blows an old cork into a celebration of party joy! Enjoy the new life of grace; trust the "forever" love of God in Christ Jesus; it is all meant for you; it is truly "joy to the world." God's Word forever shall abide.

Bibliography

Anderson, H. George, T. Austin Murphy, and Joseph A. Burgess, editors. *Justifcation by Faith, Lutherans and Catholics in Dialogue VII.* Minneapolis: Fortress,1985.

Braaten, Carl E. and Robert W. Jenson, editors. *Christian Dogmatics.* Philadelphia: Fortress, 1984.

Burgess, Joseph A., editor. *The Role of the Augsburg Confession: Catholic and Lutheran Views.* Philadelphia: Fortress, 1980.

Buechner, Frederick. *Wishful Thinking: A Theological ABC.* New York: Harper and Row, 1973.

Atkinson, Gordon. "Said the Cowboy to His People," *Christian Century Magazine,* March 7, 2005.

Forde, Gerhard O. *Justification by Faith—A Matter of Death and Life.* Philadelphia: Fortess, 1982.

Forell, George W. *The Augsburg Confession: A Contemporary Commentary.* Minneapolis: Augsburg, 1968.

Gassman, Gunther and Scott Hendrix. *Introduction to The Lutheran Confessions.* Minneapolis: Fortress, 1999.

Gritsch, Eric. "Central Pennsylvania Synod," 900 S. Arlington Ave., Harrisburg, PA: Series of monthly articles, 1980.

Gritsch, Eric. *Introduction to Lutheranism.* Minneapolis: Fortress, 1994.

Gritsch, Eric and Robert Jenson. *Lutheranism.* Philadelphia: Fortress, 1989.

Havens, Mary B. *Living Roots: A Study of the Augsburg Confession.* Minneapolis: Fortress, 1994.

Kolb, Robert and Timothy J. Wengert, translators. *The Book of Concord.* Minneapolis: Fortress, 2000.

Luther, Martin. *Luther's Works Vol. 13, Selected Psalms,* edited by Jaroslav Pelikan. St. Louis: Concordia, 1956.

———. *Luther's Works, Vol. 32, Defense and Explanation of all the Articles, 1521.* edited by Charles M. Jacobs. Philadelphia: Muhlenberg, 1958.

———. "Sermon, 1528," in *Werke*, edited by H. Bohlaus Nachfolger. Weimar Ausgabe, 1883.

Lehmann, Karl, Michael Root, and William G. Rusch, editors. *Justification by Faith.* New York: Continuum, 1997.

Steve McKinley, "Pastor Loci," *Partners Magazine,* February, 1998.

Senn, Frank. *Christian Liturgy.* Minneapolis: Fortress, 1997.